MONOGRAPH NO. 17

Thematic Relations and Transitivity in English, Japanese, and Korean

The Center for Korean Studies was established in 1972 to coordinate and develop resources for the study of Korea at the University of Hawai'i. Its goals are to enhance the quality and performance of University faculty with interests in Korean studies; to develop comprehensive and balanced academic programs relating to Korea; to stimulate research and publications on Korea; and to coordinate the resources of the University with those of the Hawai'i community and other institutions, organizations, and individual scholars engaged in the study of Korea. Reflecting the diversity of academic disciplines represented by its affiliated faculty and staff, the Center seeks especially to further interdisciplinary and intercultural studies.

Thematic Relations and Transitivity in English, Japanese, and Korean

Nam Sun Song

CENTER FOR KOREAN STUDIES
UNIVERSITY OF HAWAI'I

Copyright © 1993 by the Center for Korean Studies
University of Hawaiʻi, Honolulu, Hawaiʻi 96822

Library of Congress Cataloging-in-Publication Data

Song, Nam-Sun, 1952–
   Thematic relations and transitivity in English, Japanese, and Korean / Nam-Sun Song.
      p.   cm.
   Based on the author's thesis (Ph.D.)—University of London, 1987.
   Includes bibliographical references and index.
   ISBN 0-8248-1580-7
   1. Languages, Modern—Transitivity. 2. Languages, Modern—Semantics. 3. Languages, Modern—Topic and comment. 4. Languages, Modern—Syntax. I. Title.
PB165.T72S66   1994
401'.43—dc20   93–29693
                                                                          CIP

Contents

Preface   vii
Abbreviations   ix

Chapter 1.   Thematic Relations and Ambivalent Verbs   1

    1.   Thematic Relations   1
    1.1 The Theme with Motion Verbs   1
    1.2 The Theme with Nonmotion Verbs (Verbs of Location)   2
    1.3 Causative and Permissive Agency   3
    2.   Thematic Relations vs. Case Grammar   4
    3.   Definition of Theme   6
    4.   Alternatives   11
    4.1 Theme as the Logical Topic   12
    4.2 Factitivity and Operativity   14
    4.3 Ambivalent Verbs   17
    5.   Conclusion   22

Chapter 2.   Dative-Shift: Discourse Approaches
              vs. Semantic Approaches   25

    1.   Discourse Approaches to Dative-shift   25
    1.1 Givón's Approach   25
    1.2 Dominance and Dative Movement   26
    2.   Inadequacy of Discourse Approaches to Dative-shift   30
    2.1 English Dative-shift   30
    2.2 Word-order Variation in Japanese and Dative-shift   33
    2.3 Double-accusative Constructions in Korean   38
    3.   The Semantics of Dative-shift   43
    3.1 Ambiguity of Change in Possession   45

Chapter 3.   Double-nominative Constructions in Japanese and Korean   53

    1.   The Double-nominative Construction in Japanese   53
    1.1 The Topic–Comment Pattern and the Double-nominative   53
    1.2 Semantic Analysis of the Double-nominative   57
    1.3 Syntactic Description   65
    1.4 Conclusion: The Double-nominative in Japanese   67

2. Double-nominative Constructions in Korean   68
   2.1 Some Differences between Korean and Japanese   71
   2.2 Japanese *naru* and Korean *toy*   72
   2.3 Conclusion: Double-nominatives in Korean   81

Chapter 4.   The Passive in Japanese   83

   1. Controversy over the Japanese Passive   83
   1.1 Some Characteristics of the Japanese Passive   83
   1.2 Approaches from Relational Grammar   86
   1.2.1 Perlmutter and Postal's Universal Characterization of the Passive   86
   1.2.2 Shimizu's Proposal   87
   1.2.3 Demotional Passive   88
   1.3 Approaches from Transformational Grammar:
        Direct Passive and Indirect Passive   90
   2. Semantic Approaches to the Japanese Passive   93
   2.1 Traditional Approaches   93
   2.2 Causative Constructions and the Passive of Interest   95
   2.3 Anticausative Passive   103
   2.4 Attributive Passive   108
   2.5 Conclusion   111

Chapter 5.   Passive in Korean   113

   1. Introduction   113
   2. Transitivization   114
   3. Intransitivization   118
   3.1 Auxiliary *ci*   120
   3.2 Anticausative Passive of *ha* verbs   122
   4. Passive of Interest   125
   4.1 Passive Marking of *ha* Compound Verbs   127
   5. Attributive Passive   133

Chapter 6.   Some Typological Observations on Passives and
             Dative-Shift   135

Notes   141
References   145

Preface

This book presents a semantically oriented analysis of selected problems in the analysis of transitivity in English, Japanese, and Korean employing a system of "thematic relations" adapted from the work of Gruber and Jackendoff. A careful study of data from the three languages leads us to some modifications of this putatively universal system of semantics. The modified system is introduced in Chapter 1. One way in which it differs from those of Gruber and Jackendoff is that their ambiguous notion of Theme is replaced by two separate notions, Theme and semantic subject. Verbs are classified into "univalent verbs," which have a single set of thematic relations, and "ambivalent verbs," which have more than one set of thematic relations. It is claimed that syntactic alternations such as that between 'spray x on y' and 'spray y with x' are reflections of the ambivalence of the verbs in question.

Chapter 2 reviews discourse approaches and semantic approaches to Dative-shift. On the basis of comparative data from English and Korean, it argues that Dative-shift in these two languages is clearly a semantic process rather than a pragmatically motivated one. Moreover, like the 'spray' type alternation, Dative-shift is shown to reflect the ambivalence of verbs expressing a change in possession.

Chapter 3 is devoted to double-nominative constructions in Japanese and Korean, which in the past have been considered to be syntactically and semantically equivalent. A study of data from the two languages show that the double-nominative constructions in Korean are not homogeneous but are divided into two classes with distinct thematic relations, one of which is lacking in Japanese.

Chapters 4 and 5 discuss the passive in Japanese and Korean, respectively, and propose a new classification of passives in the two languages. Three types are recognized: the passive of interest, the anticausative passive, and the attributive passive.

Finally, Chapter 6 presents some typological observations concerning the passive and Dative-shift. In particular, the English passive and the passives of Korean and Japanese are compared with regard to their relation to

Dative-shift, and it is argued that Dative-shift and the passive are, in principle, independent grammatical processes.

This book originated as a Ph.D. thesis submitted to the University of London in January 1987. My deepest gratitude therefore goes to Dr. David C. Bennett, my thesis supervisor, who read and commented on the earlier drafts of this work. He has been a constant and patient source of advice and alternative analyses. I would also like to express my gratitude to Professor Yoshihiko Ikegami. The influence of his brilliant work is, I hope, obvious in every chapter of this book. My special thanks also go to Professor Nam In Ryang, who first introduced me to the study of languages.

In connection with the preparation of the book for publication, I should thank the following friends and colleagues: professors Hugh H. W. Kang, Ho-min Sohn, Edward J. Shultz, Chong Dal Oh, Jong Won Nam, and Mr. Joon Haeng Kim. My thanks go to my parents for their steadfast encouragement, and last, but not least, I am grateful to my wife, Chin Suk, who showed great patience during the years when I completed the earlier version of this book.

Abbreviations

Abl	=	ablative	IO	=	indirect object
Acc	=	accusative	Loc	=	locative
Adj	=	adjective	Nom	=	nominative
Aux	=	auxiliary	Pass	=	passive
Ben	=	beneficiary	Perf	=	perfect tense
Comp	=	complementizer	Pl	=	plural
Cont	=	contrastive	Pred	=	predicate
Dat	=	dative	Pres	=	present tense
DO	=	direct object	Past	=	past tense
Erg	=	ergative	Rel	=	relativizer
Gen	=	genitive	Subj	=	subject
Instr	=	instrumental	Top	=	topic

Chapter 1
Thematic Relations and Ambivalent Verbs

1. Thematic Relations

One of the most important problems in the analysis of sentence meaning is the characterization of predicates and the semantic relations that obtain between them and their arguments. One of the best-known works on this problem is Gruber (1965). Gruber posited "thematic relations," defining them as the basic structural relations at a "Prelexical" semantic level of representation. Jackendoff (1972, 1976, 1983, 1987) subsequently demonstrated that a number of problems in syntax and semantics can be satisfactorily formulated in terms of thematic relations. The fundamental semantic notion in Gruber's analysis is the Theme. While Gruber (1976)—the published version of Gruber (1965)—does not give explicit criteria for determining which NP in every sentence is the Theme, at least two points seem clear from his comments:

> The Theme also has the significance of being an obligatory element of every sentence. It appears to be the focus of the construction syntactically and semantically. (Gruber 1976:38)

According to his definition, then, the Theme is the most central element, or the focus of the construction, syntactically and semantically, and it must be present in every sentence. In Gruber (1976), although the Theme is in most cases discernible semantically, he does not explain its underlying syntactic structure or any immediate association between the Theme and any particular grammatical relations such as the subject or the direct object.

Adopting the localistic hypothesis that spatial expressions are more basic, semantically and syntactically, than various kinds of nonspatial expressions, Gruber (1976) and Jackendoff (1972) start by specifying the notion of Theme in spatial expressions and subsequently move to other more abstract domains, treating the latter as a metaphorical extension of the former.

1.1 The Theme with Motion Verbs

With verbs of motion, the Theme is defined as the NP whose referent is conceived as moving or undergoing the motion.

(1) The letter went from New York to Philadelphia.

(2) The estate went to the eldest son.

(3) The season changed from winter to spring.

In Jackendoff (1972, 1976), the semantic similarity among the above three sentences is expressed by assigning them, a common semantic representation, a function GO (x, y, z). This function designates an event consisting of the motion of x (Theme) from y (Source) to z (Goal). The important semantic difference among the three sentences is that the verbs in (2) and (3) express somewhat less concrete or more abstract motions or transitions. The difference is accounted for in terms of "parameters" (Gruber 1976), "modes" (Jackendoff 1976), or "semantic fields" (Jackendoff 1983). This differentiation is represented by means of a restrictive modifier on the semantic function, such as "Positional," "Possessional," or "Identificational." Thus given the framework presented by Jackendoff (1976), the semantic structures of (1), (2), (3) are formalized as follows:

(4) $\left[\begin{array}{l} \text{GO } (x, y, z) \\ \text{posit/poss/ident} \end{array} \right]$

1.2 The Theme with Nonmotion Verbs (Verbs of Location)

With verbs of location, the Theme is defined as the NP whose location is being asserted. Verbs of location are divided into two groups: those expressing states of affairs, as in (5), and those expressing events, as in (6).

(5) a. The statue stood on Cambridge Common.
    b. The cat lay on the couch.

(6) a. The cat stayed on the couch.
    b. Stanley remained in Africa.

The former cannot be preceded by *what happened was* while the latter can.

(7) a. *What happened was that ...
       ... the statue stood on Cambridge Common.
       ... the cat lay on the couch.
    b. What happened was that ...
       ... the cat stayed on the couch.
       ... Stanley remained in Africa.

The semantic structures taken by the verbs in (5) are represented by a semantic function BE (x, y) whereas the semantic structures taken by the verbs in (6) are represented by STAY (x, y). In either case, x stands for the Theme and y for the Location. These semantic functions appear in the same modes or semantic fields as those taken by motional verbs. The following sentences are examples of the relevant thematic relations. (The italicized NP is the Theme.)

(8) BE (x, y)
   a. *Max* is in Africa. (Positional)
   b. *The book* belongs to the library. (Possessional)
   c. *Max* is a doctor. (Identificational)

(9) STAY (x, y)
   a. *Max* stayed in Africa. (Positional)
   b. The library kept *the book* (Possessional)
   c. *Max* remained a doctor. (Identificational)

1.3 Causative and Permissive Agency

Jackendoff (1972, 1976), following Gruber, introduced two more semantic functions, CAUSE and LET, to express the semantic relations in the following sentences.

(10) a. The rock fell from the roof to the ground.
   b. Linda lowered the rock from the roof to the ground.
   c. Linda dropped the rock from the roof to the ground.

These three sentences all describe the physical motion of the rock represented by GOposit (THE ROCK, THE ROOF, THE GROUND). The semantic structures of (10b, c) are gained by adding to the semantic structure of (10a) the Agency of *Linda,* who is Causative Agent in (10b) and Permissive Agent in (10c) represented by the arguments of CAUSE and LET respectively. Thus, the thematic relations of (10b) and (10c) are represented as in (11a) and (11b).

(11) a. CAUSE (LINDA, GOposit (THE ROCK, THE ROOF, THE GROUND))
   b. LET (LINDA, GOposit (THE ROCK, THE ROOF, THE GROUND))

The thematic relations can now be defined as follows:

1. Agent is the argument of CAUSE or LET in CAUSE (x, e) or LET (x, e), where e represents an "event."

2. Theme is the element filling the first argument of the semantic functions GO (x, y, z), BE (x, y), and STAY (x, y).

3. Locative is the second element in BE (x, y) and STAY (x, y).

4. Source and Goal are the second and the third elements respectively in GO (x, y, z).[1]

The most striking theoretical contribution made by the theory of thematic relations presented by Gruber and Jackendoff must be that the theory enables us to account for syntactic and lexical regularities which otherwise appear arbitrary. For example, intuitively one does not like to say that the verb *keep* in *Herman kept the book on the shelf* and *Herman kept the book* are different verbs. Jackendoff (1983) writes as follows.

> Surely, I thought, there is no reason intrinsic to grammar that explains why the verb *keep*, for instance, can express maintenance of position *(keep the book on the shelf)*, continued possession *(keep the book)*, maintenance of property *(keep Bill angry)*, and coercion *(keep Bill working)*. Lacking a grammatical explanation, the only alternative I could imagine was that such generalization arises from the structure of the concepts the lexical and the grammatical systems express.

It seems obvious that a theory that explains this regularity is preferable to one that cannot. The theory of thematic relations, providing a semantically oriented account of otherwise arbitrary generalizations about the syntax and the lexicon, minimizes the difference between syntactic and semantic structure.

2. Thematic Relations vs. Case Grammar

Fillmore's theory of "deep cases" is roughly contemporaneous with Gruber's theory. The two theories are similar in that both of them rely heavily on the notion of semantic roles. However, what makes the theory of thematic relations distinct from Fillmore's case grammar is that the former is based on "lexical decomposition" whereas the latter is not.

In Fillmore (1988a), a number of semantic case roles are posited, for example, Agentive, Instrument, Objective, Locative, Dative, Benefactive and Factitive, and these are assigned to verbs in the form of case frames. The verb *open,* for instance, is assigned the case roles Agentive, Instrument, and Objective.

(12) a. John opened the door with a key.
 b. The key opened the door.
 c. The door opened with the key.
 d. The door opened.

The case frame for the verb *open* is +[O (I) (A)], in which Agentive and Instrument are in parentheses because they are omissible. In this theory, the assignment of case roles results in a classification of predicates. For example, *break, open, crack,* and *shatter* fall into the same class because they share a common case frame. However, Foley and Van Valin (1984:34) have correctly made the following observation.

This (case) assignment is, in an important sense, somewhat arbitrary, since it does not follow directly from the semantic structure of the predicate, which is never explicitly represented in any way.

They claim that the Gruber–Jackendoff system is more plausible than Fillmore's system since the former analysis is based on lexical decomposition. As shown in the foregoing, thematic relations are derivatives of the explicitly represented semantic structure of predicates. Thematic relations are represented formally as a function of the argument positions of abstract predicates such as CAUSE and GO. For instance, Agent is the first argument of CAUSE (x, e). Therefore, if a verb contains the abstract CAUSE in its semantic structure, the NP in the position of x is Agent.

One problem that the theory of thematic relations can deal with very well because of its property of lexical decomposition, but which Fillmore's theory cannot, is the analysis of sentences like the following.

(13) a. The rock rolled down the hill.
      b. Max rolled down the hill.

Sentence (13b) is semantically ambiguous. On one reading Max may not even be aware of his motion. On the other reading he is rolling under his own volition. In Fillmore's system, which does not admit lexical decomposition, each NP in a sentence is assigned one and only one case. Jackendoff (1972) claims any attempt to explain the ambiguity of (13b) only in terms of oppositions between the two roles Agent and Objective (or Patient) misses the fact that, even on the Agent reading, Max still undergoes the same motion as the rock in (13a). "Therefore, the similarity between two readings can be captured only if we allow Max to be both Theme and Agent on the second reading" (Jackendoff 1972:34). In Gruber's and Jackendoff's systems, noun phrases can function in more than one thematic role within the same sentence. The thematic relations of (13b) in its agentive reading are represented as follows:

CAUSE (MAX, GOposit (MAX, y, DOWN))

The thematic roles, Agent and Theme are assigned by CAUSE and GO to the same individual, *Max*.

The second difference between the theory of thematic relations and the Fillmorean case theory lies in the fact that the former is "localistic" while the latter is not. The most serious criticism of Fillmorean case theory, as Fillmore (1977) himself admits, is that no one working within the various versions of a grammar with "cases" has come up with a principled way of defining the cases, or a principled procedure for determining how many cases there are. Because of vagueness in definitions, the case inventories rely heavily upon intuitive plausibility rather than any theoretical system. In the localistic theories to which the Gruber–Jackendoff systems belong, many roles are reduced to a concrete "localistic" inventory, such as "entity to which location (or change of location) is attributed." The more abstract semantic relations are seen as a generalization of the localistic metaphor. Fillmore (1968) assigns two distinct case roles, Locative and Dative, to *Washington* in (14a) and *Mary* in (14b), respectively.

(14) a. They sent a wire to Washington.
b. They gave the prize to Mary.

In either case, however, it is plausible to assume "a motion (concrete or not) of some entity from one place to another." This assumption seems to be validated by the use of the same preposition *to* in both sentences. This commonality cannot be captured by Fillmore's case assignment. In Jackendoff's framework, (14a) and (14b) have the same thematic relations with different "parameters" or "domains" formalized as in (15).

(15) a. CAUSE (THEY, GOposit (WIRE, THEY, WASHINGTON))
b. CAUSE (THEY, GOposit (THE PRIZE, THEY, MARY))

This localistic generalization constrains the inventory of semantic roles because there is no need to introduce new roles so long as they fit into the "localistic metaphor." In the following sections, however, I will suggest that even the Gruber–Jackendoff frameworks do not escape vagueness in the definition of semantic roles.

3. Definition of Theme

As explained in Section 1, the notion of Theme that emerges from an overall consideration of Gruber's work can be characterized as in (16) and (17).

(16) The Theme is an obligatory element of a sentence and the semantic focus that the sentence is about.

(17) The Theme is the argument to which location, possession, and identity (or change of location, possession, and identity) are attributed.

One would naturally assume, from a logical point of view, that (16) is the essential criterion for recognizing the Theme, while (17) is merely its realization in a particular semantic pattern. The criteria in (16) and (17) apply fairly well to most examples Gruber and Jackendoff deal with. Sentences (18a, b, c) express changes of location, possession, and identity, respectively.

(18) a. John went to the station.
  b. The estate went to John.
  c. John went mad.

In these sentences, the most central participants, which the sentences are about in a semantic sense, are naturally the individuals that underwent changes, namely *John* in (18a), *the estate* in (18b), and *John* in (18c). In the transitive sentence (19a), the two criteria do not conflict, that is, the entity that underwent a change is also semantically the most central and obligatory element because it is the only participant that is present in all types of constructions taken by the verb, as shown in (19b) and (19c).

(19) a. John broke *the vase*.
     CAUSE (JOHN, GOident (THE VASE, *y*, BROKEN))
  b. *The vase* broke.
  c. *The vase* was broken

Many linguists have pointed out that verbs like *hit, touch, strike, slap, shoot,* and so forth are semantically distinct from verbs like *break, bend, kill, fold,* and so on. Fillmore (1970) designates the former "surface-contact" verbs and the latter "change-of-state" verbs. Sentence (19a) denotes that the direct object NP *the vase* underwent a specific change. Sentence (20a), however, does not denote that the direct object NP underwent any specific change.

(20) a. John hit the vase.
  b. *The vase hit.

Grunau (1985) points out that what is asserted about the direct object NP in (20a) is that it was "impinged-upon." The two types of verbs, which are semantically distinct, also show a syntactic difference. Verbs like *break* have intransitive forms, as in (19b), while verbs like *hit* do not. Fillmore (1968b) says that *break* is essentially a one-place predicate while *hit* is a two-place predicate. *Break,* being a one-place predicate, as in (19b), can also occur in a transitive construction like (19a) by introducing an "ergative" subject. Fillmore claims that hit, being a two-place predicate, does not show the ergative relation. Similar distinctions were drawn by Halliday (1968) between the "transitive system" and the "ergative system" and by Lyons (1977) between the "operative" construction and the "factitive" construction. Adopting Lyon's terms, we shall refer to transitive sentences like (19a) as factitive constructions and to transitive sentences like (20a) as operative constructions.

It should be noted that most of the transitive constructions Gruber and Jackendoff treat are sentences that contain a factitive verb. When the theory of thematic relations is applied to the analysis of sentences that contain an operative verb, it does not appear so promising. Jackendoff (1972:43) argues that *touch* and *hit* mark Theme in the subject, and Location or Goal in the object, but only optionally mark Agent in the subject. Thus *John* is Theme and *the car* is Goal in (21a).

(21) a. John hit the car
 b. John hit the car with the hammer.
 c. The hammer hit the car.

(22) John killed the dog (with the hammer).

In a similar way, *the hammer* is marked as Theme in (21c). As regards (21b), in Jackendoff's framework (1972, 1976), the Theme would be *the hammer* and the thematic relations of the sentence will be as in (23).

(23) CAUSE (JOHN, GOposit (THE HAMMER, JOHN, THE CAR)).

It seems plausible to claim that "what underwent a change" in (21a) is *John* or a part of his body, and in (21b, c) is *the hammer,* while *the car* is Goal in all three cases. Here, one may ask a naive question: What makes the thematic relations of (21a, b) and (22) distinct? Recall that the Theme is defined by (16) as what the sentence is semantically about, and by (17) as an entity that undergoes change in a dynamic situation. If *the dog* in (22) is the focus of the sentence, then why not *the car* in (21a). The two sentences are used to answer parallel questions: "What did John do to the car?" and "What did John do to the dog?" Furthermore, Theme, that which the sentence is semantically about, appears as an optional and peripheral element in (21b), assuming the Theme to be *the hammer*. Is that desirable? The criteria in (16) and (17) seem to conflict when they are applied to the analysis of this kind of operative construction. The two criteria seem to conflict even more seriously in the analysis of the following sentences.

(24) a. John shot Mary.
 b. John shot Mary with a bullet/with an arrow.

Sentence (24b) seems to fit well into the "localistic" pattern, as in (25), in which the Theme is *a bullet*.

(25) CAUSE (JOHN, GOposit (A BULLET, JOHN, MARY)).

But what about the Theme of (24a)? It was possible to save the theory in the case of (21a) by assigning the Theme role to the subject. However, the interpretation that the subject is "transferred" or "moved" is impossible in (24a). One could say, alternatively, that the Theme is "incorporated" into the verb or "implicitly" expressed by the verb. But how can the semantic focus that the sentence is about, and thereby a central participant, be expressed implicitly? The same problem applies to (26).

(26) a. I drained water from the pool.
b. I drained the pool of water.
c. I drained the pool.

Do (26a) and (26b) have the same thematic relations, the transfer of water from the pool to some other place? If so, is the Theme still *water* in (26c), implicitly expressed by the verb? And if these sentences have the same thematic relations, why do these distinct forms exist in a language? Gruber's and Jackendoff's theories seem to have no answer. Along the same lines, Grunau (1985) observes that the analyses by Gruber and Jackendoff cannot determine the Theme of the sentences in (27).

(27) a. Ralph gave a book to Mary.
b. Ralph gave Mary a book.
c. *Ralph gave a lot of pain to Mary.
d. Ralph gave Mary a lot of pain.

In the analyses by Gruber and Jackendoff, a book is the Theme of (27a) and (27b). However, sentence (27d) is hardly understood as an assertion about the new location of *a lot of pain*. It is, rather, about how *Mary* was affected. Is *Mary*, then, the Theme of (27d) since it is the focus that the sentence is semantically about? If the Theme of (27d) is *Mary*, the Theme of (27b) should also be *Mary*, because *Mary* is affected by the action there as well. Grunau says that the questions are endless.

Criticism may come from another angle. Ikegami (1981b) points out that in the following sentences with a preposition, the semantic focus is on "action" whereas in those without prepositions the semantic focus is on "achievement."

(28) a. John hit the car.
b. John hit at the car.

(29) a. John pushed the car.
b. John pushed against the car.

(30) a. John grasped a straw.
b. John grasped at a straw.

Ikegami also reports that (31a) is contradictory, while (31b) is not.

(31) a. *I kicked John, but I didn't get him.
b. I kicked at John, but I didn't get him.

This fact supports the view that (31a) emphasizes "achievement" while (31b) emphasizes "action." There is further evidence that supports Ikegami's view. Many operative verbs can be used as factitive verbs, such as *shoot* in (32a) and *knock* in (33a).

(32) a. John shot Mary dead.
 b. *John shot at Mary dead.

(33) a. John knocked the door down.
 b. *John knocked on the door down.

In order for the goal to which the action is directed to undergo a change in state, the action has to be first "achieved." The ill-formedness of (32b) and (33b) can be accounted for thus: expressions that emphasize "action" cannot be used as factitive expressions because they do not guarantee "achievement," which is a prerequisite to the factitive reading. This analysis also provides a good account of why English has alternative forms like (28)–(30), while the Gruber–Jackendoff approach provides no account of them.

Given the analysis that in the above sentences with prepositions the semantic focus is on "action" while in the prepositionless sentences it is on "achievement," it seems fully warranted to assume that the former sentences are semantically about the actions of "actors" or "agents," so that by criterion (16) "actors" or "agents" are the Theme; while the latter sentences are about the "affectedness" of "patients" or "goals," making them the Theme. It is obvious by now that, in the analysis of an operative sentence, the two criteria in (16) and (17) are in total conflict. As already pointed out, the second criterion is from a logical viewpoint merely the realization of the first one in a particular semantic pattern. However, what is important, as shown clearly in the discussion so far, is that Gruber and Jackendoff in practice abandon criterion (16)—that the Theme is that which the sentence is semantically about—when the two criteria conflict and narrow down the definition of Theme to one of the semantic roles, that is, the participant to which location or change of location is attributed. Consequently, the theory of thematic relations has no explanatory power in the analysis of sentences whose meaning can hardly be reduced to a localistic pattern.

The second inadequacy of the theory of thematic relations is that it does not offer any proper description of the meanings of the syntactic variants taken by the same verbs. Anderson (1977), criticizing Fillmore's position, points out the important semantic difference between sentences like (24a) and (34b).

(34) a. John painted the white paint on the wall.
 b. John painted the wall with the white paint.

Sentence (34a) implies that the white paint is used up, though the wall may not have been covered, whereas (34b) implies that there may well be some paint left, though the wall was completely covered. In a Gruber or Jackendoff framework, however, one can only say that (34a) and (34b) have the same thematic relations (*the white paint* = Theme, *the wall* = Goal) with different surface structures.

A third deficiency now emerges from the argument so far. It is noticeable that the semantic differences pointed out in (28)–(30) and (34) correspond to the syntactic positions taken by the NPs in question: direct object position or object of a preposition. Gruber and Jackendoff never specify the relations between particular thematic roles and particular grammatical relations in spite of the fact that, in the majority of the examples which they adduce, the Theme appears either as the subject or the direct object. It follows from this that they have no explanation of the systematic correspondence between meaning and form. One of the most striking theoretical contributions made by Gruber and Jackendoff, as already pointed out, is that they put a constraint on semantic theory: requiring that any adequate semantic theory be able to account for syntactic and lexical regularities that otherwise appear arbitrary. This constraint is referred to in Jackendoff (1983) as the "Grammatical Constraint" on semantics. However, with regard to the relation between thematic roles and grammatical relations, Jackendoff clearly does not observe this constraint and shares with most Fillmorean theories their undesirable arbitrariness as regards the relationship between semantic structures and syntactic forms.[2]

4. Alternatives

The discussion so far suggests some characteristics that a more preferable semantic theory of the sentence should contain:

(35) a. The theory should provide a systematic account of operative sentences as well as factitive sentences, and should incorporate a solution to the aforementioned problems involved in defining the notion Theme.

b. The theory has to contain principles whose application allows us to explain syntactic variants taken by the same verb, such as (27)–(39) and (34a, b).

c. The theory has to specify how such grammatical relations as subject and direct object relate to semantic roles.

4.1 Theme as the Logical Topic

Anderson (1977) proposes a characterization of the Theme as the "logical topic."

> In a sense, the Theme is the "logical topic" of the clause: the element that the clause is about, in a purely logical sense divorced from any particular use of the clause in discourse. This sort of logical topicality must be kept rigorously distinct from discourse topicality: thus, while a sentence such as *John took his books back to the library* could be used in discourse to make a statement about John (*Where did he go?*), the books (*What happened to the ones that were on this desk?*), the library (*Why are all of its shelves full suddenly?*), it is still a statement about the books, in a logical sense, whose motion or location are described independently of such discourse factors. (Anderson 1977:367)

With a motion verb, the Theme as logical topic is the entity that moves; with a verb specifying location, it is the entity whose location is thus defined; with many transitive verbs, it is the Patient or entity that undergoes the action. Anderson claims that, just as the agent relation is consistently associated with the syntactic position of subject, the Theme is normally associated with the subject of an intransitive verb and the direct object of a transitive verb. The consistent association obtaining between the semantic notions and the grammatical relations is referred to in terms of the "Agent-rule" and the "Theme-rule." Anderson maintains that the Agent-rule and Theme-rule, owing to their overwhelming regularity, significantly simplify the lexical redundancy rules. In Jackendoff (1976), the relation between the thematic roles and their syntactic positions has to be stated in the lexical entry of every verb. For example, the lexical representation for *melt* in its intransitive use is as in (36).

(36) $\begin{bmatrix} /\text{melt}/ \\ +V \\ +[\text{NP1} \_\_] \\ \text{GOident (NP1, SOLID, LIQUID)} \end{bmatrix}$ (Jackendoff 1976:103)

The index number given to the NP represents the association of the Theme with the subject position. However, with the Theme-rule the association is automatically decided and does not need to be specified in every lexical entry.

The semantic differences between the alternative forms in (37) and (38) are also stated by the Theme-rule.

(37) a. John painted my picture this morning.
    b. John painted on my picture this morning.

(38) a. A vandal smeared the paint on my house.
b. A vandal smeared my house with the paint.

Anderson argues that the direct object NPs in the (a) sentences are interpreted as completely or "holistically" affected, while the prepositional objects are interpreted as "partially" affected. It is assumed, moreover, that if an NP occupying the direct object position is shifted into some other structural position, it ceases to be the Theme. Anderson argues that it is this change in thematic relations that causes the semantic difference found in the pairs in (37) and (38).

Anderson's work is an attempt to solve the problems of the theory of thematic relations pointed out in (35). He defines the Theme only as in (16), as the logical topic, that is, the element that the sentence is semantically about. Hence, not only the direct object NP of a factitive verb, such as *the vase* in (39a), but also the direct object NP of an operative verb, such as *the vase* in (39b), is analyzed as a Theme.

(39) a. I broke the vase.
b. I hit the vase.

The syntactic alternatives allowed by the same verb, as in (38), which are assumed to have the same thematic relations in Gruber–Jackendoff's analysis, are now assigned different thematic relations, and the semantic difference between them is attributed to the difference in their thematic relations. The syntactic distribution of the Theme is specified as the subject of an intransitive construction and the direct object of a transitive construction.

Anderson's solution, however, is too sketchy to be an alternative to the theory of thematic relations proposed by Gruber and Jackendoff. His definition of the Theme as the logical topic also does not eliminate the vagueness of the notion Theme. It is not clear whether the Theme as the logical topic is still a semantic role like Locative, Goal, and so forth, or a notion on a distinct level. If the Theme is a semantic role, what is the relation between the Theme and Patient? Anderson says that with many transitive verbs the Theme is Patient, as in (39b). If so, is the direct object NP of (39b) assigned two semantic roles, while the direct object NP of (39a) is assigned only the one rule of Theme? Alternatively, if the Theme is no longer a semantic role but a notion on a different level, the direct object NP of (39b) is defined as the Theme with the semantic role Patient. In this case, what semantic role does the direct object NP of (39a) have? Anderson's proposal seems far from providing a solution to the vagueness of the notion Theme. What is common to Gruber–Jackendoff and Anderson is that they use the term Theme ambiguously: sometimes as the semantic focus (or logical topic) that the sentence is about, and sometimes as a semantic role, the entity that has a specific location, ownership, or identity, or the entity that undergoes change of location, ownership, or identity. Gruber and Jackendoff give priority to the latter and Anderson to the former. I think that the vagueness of the notion of Theme stems from this ambiguity. I also think that there is no intrinsic reason why one has to assume that the logical topic or the semantic focus that the sentence is about should be consistently associated with the semantic role of the entity that is in a specific state or that undergoes a specific change. These two facets could be characterized as two notions that are independent of each other.

4.2 Factitivity and Operativity

We have so far argued that the criteria in (16) and (17) do not necessarily coincide, in other words, that we are dealing with two independent notions. Therefore from now on we use the term "semantic subject" as a label for the notion involved in (16), reserving the term "Theme" for the notion involved in (17). See Bennett (1975:14–15) for a similar use of the term "semantic subject." The participant referred to by the term semantic subject is unique in two ways. First, if there is any participant that is represented in all types of sentences allowed by a given predicate, this is it. Second, this participant is semantically the most neutral one. Bennett (1975:14) writes:

> What this means is that the participant with this function in a given proposition is shown thereby merely to be in some way involved. The exact nature of the involvement depends on whatever other functions are represented, i.e., on the type of sentence.

In a particular sentence, the semantic subject is realized as an obligatory participant about which the rest of the sentence asserts semantic information. It is quite natural to assume that the semantic subject, being an obligatory participant, is realized as a core syntactic element, that is, the subject or the direct object of a sentence. It is also natural that the semantic subject, being semantically the most neutral element, occurs in a core syntactic position because other syntactic positions are strongly associated with their inherent semantic content.

In an intransitive construction, the semantic subject (SS) is realized as the subject NP. For instance, in (40a) the semantic subject is *John* and its semantic nature is specified by the rest of the sentence as the participant to be located, namely, the Theme. Similarly, in (40b) and (40c) the semantic subjects are specified as entities in an abstract location.

(40) a. John   is   in his room.
       SS = Theme   Locative

   b. The book   belongs   to John.
       SS = Theme   Locative

   c. John   is   happy.
       SS = Theme   Locative

In (41), the semantic subjects are identified by the rest of each sentence as entities that undergo a change (of position, possession, and condition[3] respectively).

(41) a. The letter   went   from London   to Leeds.
       SS = Theme   Source   Goal

   b. The estate   went   to the eldest son.
       SS = Theme   Goal

   c. The season   changes   from winter   to spring.
       SS = Theme   Source   Goal

The thematic relations of the sentences in (40) and (41) are formalized as the functions (42a) and (42b) respectively.

(42) a. BEposit/poss/cond (x, y)
    b. GOposit/poss/cond (x, y, z)

In a transitive construction containing a factitive verb like *break*, the semantic subject is the participant occurring in the direct object position, because this participant is the only obligatory element represented in all other types of constructions taken by the verb.

(43) a. John broke *the vase*.
    b. John broke *the vase* with the stick.
    c. The stick broke *the vase*.
    d. *The vase* broke.
    e. *The vase* was broken.

A transitive construction containing an operative verb like *hit* also marks the semantic subject in the direct object position since this participant is shared by all other types of constructions taken by the verb.

(44) a. John hit *the vase*.
    b. John hit *the vase* with the stick.
    c. The stick hit *the vase*.
    d. *The vase* was hit.

In (43a), a factitive construction, the semantic nature of the verb confers on the semantic subject, *the vase*, the information that it underwent a change of condition. However, we cannot say that *the vase* in (44a) underwent a change in condition. It is simply "directly operated-upon." Our claim is thus that operative constructions like (44a) primarily denote that the Agent directly operates upon some entity, and that the semantic structure of (44a) cannot be described in terms of change to the Theme. We assign the traditional term "Patient" to the participant that is simply operated-upon by the Agent. Sentence (43a) and (44a) are analyzed as follows:

(45) a. John   broke   the vase.   (Factive)
        Agent   SS = Theme

     b. John   hit   the vase.   (Operative)
        Agent   SS = Patient

The semantic structure of (43a) is formalized as in (46).

(46)   CAUSE (JOHN, GOcond (THE VASE, y, BROKEN))

Since we consider that the operative sentence (44a) denotes that the Agent directly operates upon the Patient, its semantic structure is not decomposable into "causation" by an Agent and "change" to a Theme. Therefore we assign it the semantic representation in (47), which does not contain an "embedded" proposition.

(47)   Predicate (x, y) $(x = $ Agent, $y = $ Patient$)$

The semantic structure of (44a) is represented as in (48).

(48)   HIT (JOHN, THE VASE)

Our formalization need not reflect the distribution of the semantic subject. Once we know whether the predicate is factitive or operative, the distribution of the semantic subject is decided. Assigning the factitive representation CAUSE $(w, $ GO $(x, y, z))$ means that x is the semantic subject and that it is given the semantic role Theme. Similarly, assigning the operative representation Predicate (x, y) means that y is the semantic subject and Patient.

This analysis captures an important generalization about the relation between the semantic structure of a sentence and its syntactic form. In dynamic transitive constructions, the semantic subject is the participant occurring in the direct object position and is identified either as Theme or Patient, depending on whether the sentence is factitive or operative. We need no longer say that the participant with the semantic role Theme, which is also the semantic focus, occurs sometimes in the subject position, sometimes in the direct object position, sometimes in a peripheral position, and sometimes not at all.

We have so far criticized the assumption made by Gruber and Jackendoff that every participant of a sentence is characterized either as figure (Theme) or ground (Locative, Source, Goal, etc.) and that every type of construction is semantically about the Theme. The position taken here is that the localistic hypothesis accounts for syntactic and semantic regularities to a considerable extent, but not all the time. Our claim may be referred to as a "weak localistic hypothesis" while the assumption shared by Gruber and Jackendoff may be referred to as a "strong localistic hypothesis."

4.3 Ambivalent Verbs

In our analysis, verbs are either univalent or ambivalent.[4] Univalent verbs have only one set of thematic relations. Examples of the first type of ambivalent verb are listed in (49).

(49) strike, hit, kick, catch, seize, grasp, knock, etc.

A typical situation denoted by the verb *strike* is analyzable from two points of view: one is that the agent performs an operation upon an object, and the other is that the agent moves a fist or other instrument to the object. The former aspect of the meaning fits into the "operative" pattern while the latter fits into the "factitive" pattern. They can be represented as follows:

(50) a. STRIKE (w, z) (Operative)
      b. CAUSE $(w, \text{GOposit}(x, y, z))$ (Factitive)

In the operative reading, the semantic subject is Patient (z), while in the factitive reading it is Theme (x). The two readings are not on an equal footing, however. Logically, (50b) is a prerequisite to (50a). This relation is formalized by putting the prerequisite reading on the left of the other, as in (51).

(51) strike: Factitive and Operative.

Our assumption is that, between the two readings allowed by an ambivalent verb, only one of them can be semantically emphasized. The ambivalence stipulated in (51) corresponds to the following examples.

(52) a. He struck his fist upon the table. (Factitive emphasized)
   Agent   SS = Theme   Goal

b. He struck the table with his fist. (Operative emphasized)
   Agent   SS = Theme   Instrument

The semantic structures of these two sentences are represented as in (53a) and (53b) respectively.

(53) a. CAUSE (HE, GOposit (HIS FIST, y, THE TABLE))
b. STRIKE WITH HIS FIST (HE, THE TABLE)

In (52b), the operative reading that he performed an operation upon the table is emphasized. In such a case, *his fist*, which is interpreted as Theme in (52a), is likely to be interpreted as an instrument with which the Agent performs an operation upon the Patient. The verb *hit* has the same ambivalence as *strike*.

(54) a. John hit the cane against the wall. (Factitive emphasized)
   CAUSE (JOHN, GOposit (THE CANE, y, THE WALL))
b. John hit the wall with the cane. (Operative emphasized)
   HIT WITH THE CANE (JOHN, THE WALL)

The movement represented by GO (x, y, z) has two subtypes, although our formalization does not reflect the distinction. They can be represented by 'x GO TO z' and 'x GO TOWARD z'. The former necessarily entails that x has contact with z, while the latter does not. The Goal of the latter type of movement is typically marked by the prepositions *toward* and *at*. The verb *shoot* has almost the same ambivalence as *strike* and *hit* but it expresses only the "*toward*-type" movement in a factitive-emphasized construction.

(55) a. John shot the bullet at the man. (Factitive emphasized)
   CAUSE (JOHN, GOposit (THE BULLET, y, THE MAN))
b. John shot the man with the bullet. (Operative emphasized)
   SHOOT WITH THE BULLET (JOHN, THE MAN)

In a sentence denoting directed action in which the Theme is unspecified, the Agent is broadly interpreted as Theme. Then the opposition between factitive-emphasized and operative-emphasized is present as the syntactic opposition between the intransitive and transitive constructions, as follows:

(56) a. John struck upon the table. (Factitive emphasized)
   b. John struck the table. (Operative emphasized)

(57) a. John hit against the wall. (Factitive emphasized)
   b. John hit the wall. (Operative emphasized)

The sentences in (57) are analyzed as follows:

(58) a. John   hit   against the wall.   (Factitive emphasized)
        SS = Agent+Theme   Goal
     b. John   hit   the wall.   (Operative emphasized)
        Agent   SS = Patient

The second type of ambivalent verbs are those like *paint, load, spray, drain,* and *empty*. In the frameworks proposed by Gruber and Jackendoff, it is assumed that every verb is assigned a single set of thematic relations. This assumption is basically adopted by Foley and Van Valin (1984) and Grunau (1985). The following alternative forms are, in the frameworks of Gruber and Jackendoff, considered to have the same thematic relations.

(59) a. John painted white paint on the wall.
     b. John painted the wall with white paint.
     c. CAUSE (JOHN, GOposit (WHITE PAINT, y, THE WALL))

(60) a. John loaded the hay onto the truck.
     b. John loaded the truck with the hay.
     c. CAUSE (JOHN, GOposit (THE HAY, y, THE TRUCK))

(61) a. John drained water from the pool.
     b. John drained the pool of water.
     c. CAUSE (JOHN, GOposit (WATER, THE POOL, z))

(62) a. John emptied water from the glass.
     b. John emptied the glass of water.
     c. CAUSE (JOHN, GOposit (WATER, THE GLASS, z))

We consider that a semantic theory should motivate these alternations. Gruber and Jackendoff, treating the alternative forms as being semantically equivalent, cannot explain why English has such alternative syntactic forms. Second, their frameworks cannot provide any account of why some verbs can have such alternative forms as those in (59)–(62) while some cannot, in spite of the fact that they have the same thematic relations.

(63) a. John put the hay on the truck.
     b. *John put the truck with the hay.
     c. CAUSE (JOHN, GOposit (THE HAY, y, TRUCK))

(64) a. John removed the table from the room.
     b. *John removed the room of the table.
     c. CAUSE (JOHN, GOposit (THE TABLE, THE ROOM, z))

Put and *remove* express only the positional changes that their direct object NPs undergo and express nothing about the conditional change that the Goal or the Source may undergo as a consequence of the positional change. It follows that *put* and *remove* are purely positional in their semantic content and, therefore, univalent. This is why they do not have syntactic variants like (63b) and (64b). In contrast, verbs like *load, drain, empty,* and *paint* seem to describe two distinct changes. For instance, *drain*, unlike *remove*, entails that the entity denoted by the Source NP undergoes a specific change of condition as a consequence of the positional change of some other entity. The two changes expressed by *drain* can be represented as follows.

(65) a. CAUSE (w, GOposit (x, y, z)) (Factitive 1)
 b. CAUSE (w, GOcond (y, u, EMPTY)) (Factitive 2)

Drain is ambivalent between the two factitive readings. The ambivalence of *drain* is stipulated as follows:

(66) drain: Factitive 1 and Factitive 2

Given the analysis proposed above, the semantic structure of the sentences in (61) are analyzed as follows.

(67) a. John drained water from the pool. (Factitive 1 emphasized)
 CAUSE (JOHN, GOposit (WATER, THE POOL, z))

 b. John drained the pool of water. (Factitive 2 emphasized)
 CAUSE (JOHN, GOcond (THE POOL, y, EMPTY OF WATER))

Thus we abandon the assumption that each verb is given only a single set of thematic relations. The analysis proposed above is superior to those by Gruber, Jackendoff, Foley and Van Valin, and Grunau in that it provides a semantic account, based on an explicit characterization of verbs, of why the syntactic alternations in (59)–(62) are lexically conditioned. Some explanations will be necessary about *water* in (61b) and (67b). In our analysis it is not given a semantic role in the reading referred to as Factitive 2. The verb *drain* already has the Goal of the conditional change in its semantic content as specified in (65b). Therefore, *of water* in (61b) is analyzed as a further specification of the Goal expressed by the verb. This is why *of water* in (61b) is omissible.

(68) a. John drained the pool.
 b. CAUSE (JOHN, GOcond (THE POOL, y, EMPTY))

The verbs *paint, load,* and *empty* have almost the same ambivalence as *drain*, represented as follows.

(69) paint: CAUSE (w, GOposit (x, y, z)) (Factitive 1)
 CAUSE (w, GOcond (z, u, PAINTED WITH x)) (Factitive 2)

(70) load: CAUSE (w, GOposit (x, y, z)) (Factive 1)
CAUSE (w, GOcond (z, u, FILLED WITH x)) (Factive 2)
(71) empty: CAUSE (w, GOposit (x, y, z)) (Factive 1)
CAUSE (w, GOcond (y, u, EMPTY OF x)) (Factive 2)

Drain and *empty* have the same thematic relations and almost the same ambivalence, but differ in the manner in which their Goals of the conditional changes are specified. *Drain* has the selectional restriction that the 'content' has to be an entity that can 'flow'.

(72) a. John drained the pool of water.
b. John drained me of energy.

On the other hand, *empty* does not have such a restriction, as shown in (73).

(73) John emptied the closet of all its things.

Anderson (1977), as already mentioned, claims that in (74a) and (74b) the postverbal NPs are interpreted "holistically," while the NPs with prepositions are interpreted "partitively."

(74) a. John painted the white paint on the wall.
b. John painted the wall with the white paint.

However, to claim that the essential difference between alternative forms of this type lies in the contrast between "partitive" and "holistic" interpretations is an oversimplifications. Whether an NP is interpreted partitively or holistically varies according to definiteness of the NP. Compare (60) and (75).

(75) a. John loaded hay onto the truck.
b. John loaded the truck with hay.

The definite NP *the hay* is likely to be interpreted holistically either in (60a) or (60b). If *the hay* in (60b) were to be given a partitive interpretation, one would say either (75b) or (76).

(76) John loaded the truck with some of the hay.

By contrast, the indefinite NP *hay* is interpreted partitively either in (75a) or (75b). What is certain about the semantic difference between alternative forms of this type, as pointed out by Ikegami (1981b), is that the direct object NP is interpreted as being affected more greatly or seriously when it occurs as direct object than when it occurs in a peripheral syntactic position. This is quite compatible with our analysis. Each alternative form in (59)–(62) emphasizes the change undergone by the direct object NP, that is, the semantic subject. Thus it is quite likely to be interpreted as being more greatly affected than when it is not the semantic subject.

Another set of data supporting our analysis is from Williams (1980). The predication relation holds between the italicized NPs and the italicized adjective phrases in the following examples.

(77) a. *John* is *sad*.
b. John ate *the meat raw*.
c. *John* ate the meat *nude*.
d. John made *Bill mad*.

Williams (1980) says that the predication relation holds only if the NP c-commands and is c-subjacent to the modifying AP. He holds that the c-command restriction can be seen in the following examples.

(78) a. John loaded *the wagon full* with hay.
b. John loaded *the hay* into the wagon *green*.
c. *John loaded the wagon with *hay green*.
d. *John loaded the hay into the *wagon full*.

The predication relation does not hold in (78c) because *hay* does not c-command *green,* contained inside a PP that does not contain *green*. In (78d), *the wagon* does not c-command *full*.

This strictly syntactic analysis is compatible with our semantic analysis. Sentences (78a) and (78b) are semantically about the respective changes undergone by *the wagon* and *the hay,* and therefore the Goals of their conditional changes can be spelled out explicitly. However, in (78c) and (78d), which are semantically about the changes to the direct object NPs, the APs cannot be interpreted as the Goals of the changes in condition undergone by the oblique NPs.

5. Conclusion

We have discussed our alternative to the frameworks proposed by Gruber and Jackendoff. Our framework is preferable for three reasons. First of all, while inheriting all the useful localistic generalizations about syntactic and lexical regularities, it provides at the same time an account of the syntactic regularities shared by the factitive and operative constructions. Second, in our framework, the Theme, a notion used ambiguously by Gruber and Jackendoff, is replaced by two separate notions, for one of which the label "Theme" is retained, while the other is that of the "semantic subject" of a sentence. This distinction enabled us to specify explicitly the relationship between the semantic structure of a sentence and the core grammatical relations, that is, the subject and the direct object. Third, our analysis of verbs into univalent and ambivalent verbs provides more plausible and systematic explanations of the *paint*-type syntactic alternation.

Chapter 2
Dative-Shift: Discourse Approaches vs. Semantic Approaches

Many works have been devoted to the syntactic description of Dative-shift in English.[1] However, comparatively little attention has been paid to why English has such a syntactic alternation. In this chapter, the discourse approaches proposed by Givón (1979, 1990) and Erteschik-Shir (1979) are examined and criticized. It is claimed that the Dative-shift rules in English and Korean are semantic processes.

1. Discourse Approaches to Dative-shift

1.1 Givón's Approach

Givón (1979), examining data from a variety of languages, proposed an analysis of Dative-shift in terms of the following two features, each of which is familiar from earlier analyses.

(1) The erstwhile indirect object loses its case-marking morpheme.

(2) The order of two objects is reversed.

Givón says that the "demoted" accusative object may remain unmarked when the prepositional object is Dative or Benefactive as in (3), while it may otherwise acquire a preposition, as in (4).

(3) a. John gave a book to Mary.
    b. John gave Mary a book.

(4) a. John sprayed paint on the wall.
    b. John sprayed the wall with paint.

The type of alternation in (4) may also be thought of as Dative-shift from a functional viewpoint. Of the two features of Dative-shift, Givón takes (2) as the essential feature, while regarding (1) as a feature specific to SVO languages like English. He argues that the most common function of the Dative-shift is changing the "relative topicality" of the accusative vis-à-vis the prepositional object.

This involves the universal word-order principle that the left-most constituent is the "more topical" one, that is, the one more likely to not constitute new information (Givón 1979:161).

He claims that his assumption is compatible with the following data.

(5) a. When he found it, John gave the book to Mary.
    b. ?When he found it, John gave Mary the book.
(6) a. When he found her, John gave Mary the book.
    b. ?When he found her, John gave the book to Mary.

In (5), the accusative object is established as topical via previous mention in a preposed topical adverbial clause and, therefore, Acc–Dat is more natural. Dat–Acc is more natural in (6) since the dative object is established as topical.

Givón holds that the type of Dative-shift which involves both (1) and (2) is restricted to SVO languages. However, he claims that from a functional viewpoint Dative-shift exists in SOV languages too.

> One can also show that the same rule of dative-shift, in functional terms, may also exist in an SOV language where no morphological changes in the case marking are associated with it, but only the relative order change (Givón 1979:153).

He adduces the following examples from Sherpa, a Tibeto-Burman language.

(7) tiki   kitabi   coxts-i-kha-la   zax-sung
    he-Erg   book   table-Gen-on-Dat   put-Aux
    'He put the book on the table.'

(8) tiki   coxts-i-kha-la   kitabi   zax-sung
    he-Erg   table-Gen-on-Dat   book   put-Aux
    'He put on the table a book.'

When the previous context topicalizes the accusative object, as in *I asked him what he did with the book, so he said that ...*, the order Acc–Dat is preferred while if the dative is topicalized, the order Dat–Acc is preferred. Thus, Givón assumes that Dative-shift in SVO languages and the relative word-order change in SOV languages perform an identical function.

1.2 Dominance and Dative Movement

Erteschik-Shir (1979) claims that Dative movement (another term for Dative-shift) in English is best accounted for not in syntax but in terms of discourse constraints. A notion of "dominance," is posited to explain the discourse functions of Dative Movement. The definition of "dominance" follows.

(9) Dominance: A constituent C of a sentence S is dominant in S if and only if the speaker intends to direct the attention of his hearers to the intension of C by uttering S. (443)

A dominant constituent therefore is the natural candidate for the topic of further conversation as in (10).

(10) Speaker A: I saw Picasso's picture of the blue angel yesterday.
Speaker B: Oh, yes, I know which one it is.

The pronoun it in (10) can only refer to Picasso's picture of the blue angel and not to the blue angel. It indicates that only the larger NP is dominant in A's utterance.

The dominance relation is related to various determiners and to degree of specificity, as tested in (11)–(16).

(11) Speaker A: John killed a cop.
Speaker B: Oh, yes, I know which one it is.

(12) Speaker A: John killed the cop who was a criminal himself.
Speaker B: Oh, yes, I know which one it is.

(13) Speaker A: John killed the cop.
Speaker B: ?Oh, yes, I know which one it is.

(14) Speaker A: John killed the president.
Speaker B: ?Oh, yes, I know which one it is.

(15) Speaker A: John killed Howie.
Speaker B: *Oh, yes, I know which Howie it is.

(16) Speaker A: John killed him.
Speaker B: **Oh, yes, I know who he is.

There is a hierarchy according to which indefinites are generally used to indicate that an NP is dominant, while definites generally indicate that an NP is nondominant, and pronouns cannot possibly be used dominantly. It is pointed out, however, that there are instances of a definite NP being interpreted dominantly. Such pronouns as *him* or *her* can also receive a dominant interpretation, providing they are stressed. However, this is not normal. It is claimed that these facts make the notion of dominance distinct from the well-known notion of focus or new information. The notion of dominance is assumed also to be distinct from communicative dynamism, because the latter is a relative notion while the former is an absolute property. There is only one NP that cannot be used dominantly, that is *it*. Thus, *it* is thought of as the archetype of the nondominant NP. Erteschik-Shir proposed a rule for Dative Movement as shown in (17).

(17) In the structure ... V NP$_1$ NP$_2$ (derived from ... V NP$_2$ to/for NP$_1$)
NP$_1$ is nondominant and NP$_2$ is dominant.

The following data are adduced to support the hypothesis in (17). The preferred order is marked a plus sign (+).

(18) a. John gave a book to Mary.
b. +John gave Mary a book.

(19) a. John gave a book to the girl.
b. +John gave the girl a book.

(20) a. John gave a book to her.
b. +John gave her a book.

(21) a. +John gave the book to Mary.
b. John gave Mary the book.

In (18)–(20), rule (17) places the indefinite NP in the final position in the (b) sentences, where it is more easily interpreted as being dominant. Therefore, the (b) version is preferred, since the rule has applied. In (21), the underlying order is preferred since the more dominant NP already follows the less dominant in it. Erteschik-Shir claims that the validity of the rule is clearer on the basis of the aforementioned dominance test.

(22) Speaker A: John gave a book to someone yesterday.
Speaker B: Oh, yes, I know who it was.

(23) Speaker A: John gave someone a book yesterday.
Speaker B: *Oh, yes, I know who it was.
Oh, yes, I know which one it was.

In (22) the response can refer either to the *someone* or the *book*, while in (23) the response can only refer to the *book*; that is, *someone* cannot be interpreted as being dominant after Dative Movement has applied.

> The test thus strengthens the analysis of Dative Movement as a rule that functions to force a dominant interpretation on the NP that ends up in final position (and a nondominant interpretation on the other NP) (Erteschik-Shir 1979:451).

The following exceptions have been problematic for syntactic approaches to Dative-shift.

(24) a. John gave it to Mary.
　　 b) *John gave Mary it.

(25) a. Who did John give the book to?
　　 b. *Who did John give the book?

Erteschik-Shir argues that the discourse approach can solve these problems. *It* cannot occur in the rightmost position in double-object constructions as in (26)–(29).

(26) a. John gave it to a girl.
　　 b. *John gave a girl it.

(27) a. John gave it to the girl.
　　 b. *John gave the girl it.

(28) a. John gave it to Mary.
　　 b. *John gave Mary it.

(29) a. John gave it to her.
　　 b. *John gave her it.

As already pointed out, *it* can never be interpreted as being dominant. It is maintained that the (b) sentences are ill-formed because Dative Movement assigns dominance to an NP that cannot be interpreted as dominant.

The discourse rule also provides an account of the unacceptability of (30) and (31).

(30) *Who did John give the book?

(31) *The girl that John gave the book is very nice.

What causes the unacceptability of these sentences is that, in each case, an NP is highlighted by means of questioning and relativization and thus given dominance, while at the same time Dative Movement forces nondominant interpretations on the NP in question.

The discourse rule also explains the following data.

(32) *John told that he liked ice cream to Mary.

(33) John told Mary that he liked ice cream.

Erteschik-Shir says that sentential complement and "heavy NPs," due to their length, must be interpreted as being dominant and are therefore preferred in sentence-final position.

Thus, Erteschik-Shir concludes that a discourse analysis of Dative Movement predicts various kinds of data that other analyses find it difficult to account for.

2. Inadequacy of Discourse Approaches to Dative-shift

The discourse approaches to Dative-shift proposed by Givón and Erteschik-Shir are a considerable improvement on simply writing a syntactic transformation and not bothering to ask about the circumstances under which each variant is used. However, this section refutes the claim that Dative-shift is a process that primarily serves discourse functions, on two grounds: (a) it cannot explain the problem of exceptions, and (b) a change in topicality or change in "dominance" tied to word-order change is not inherent in Dative-shift.

2.1 English Dative-shift

Three properties have been pointed out by many linguists with regard to the Dative-shift in English. First, it is highly lexically conditioned. For instance, *teach* and *explain* are somewhat similar to each other, but only the former allows Dative-shift.

(34) a. John taught the story to Bill.
 b. John taught Bill the story.

(35) a. John explained the story to Bill.
 b. *John explained Bill the story.

(36) a. John told the story to Bill.
 b. John told Bill the story.

(37) a. John said these words to Bill.
 b. *John said Bill these words.

(38) a. John sent some stock to Bill.
 b. John sent Bill some stock.

(39) a. John transferred some stock to Bill.
 b. *John transferred Bill some stock.

Second, the "shifted" indirect object normally has to be animate.

(40) a. John brought the piano to New York.
 b. *John brought New York the piano.

(41) a. John brought the piano to Bill.
 b. John brought Bill the piano.

Third, the structure with a preposition is not allowed when the direct object NPs denote "diseases" or certain other abstract entities.

(42) a. *Mary gave the measles to John.
 b. Mary gave John the measles.

(43) a. *Mary gave an inferiority complex to John.
     b. Mary gave John an inferiority complex.
(44) a. *Mary gave a broken arm to John.
     b. Mary gave John a broken arm.
(45) a. *Mary gave a pain in the neck to John.
     b. Mary gave John a pain in the neck.

Dative-shift is optional in (34), (36), (38), and (41), while it is blocked in (35), (37), (39), and (40), and is obligatory in (42)–(45). None of these three restrictions seem to have a clear discourse motivation. The Dative Movement rule in (17) proposed by Erteschik-Shir does not provide any account of these restrictions. Note that the notion of dominance is defined in terms of the speaker's intention. A constituent is dominant if the speaker intends to direct the attention of his hearers to an entity denoted by the constituent. In other words, dominance is a relation that holds between the speaker's intention and the entity denoted by an NP. The notion of dominance and the rule based on it, therefore, can say nothing about why Dative-shift is allowed with *teach* and not with *explain*. Rule (17) also cannot explain the animacy constraint on the indirect object NPs in (40) and (41) because there is no reason why the speaker could not intend to direct the attention of his hearers to *New York*. Erteschik-Shir says that there is no condition on Dative Movement that makes the transformation obligatory with diseases, adducing the following examples.

(46) a. John gave Mary pneumonia and he gave it to Ted too.
     b. *John gave Mary pneumonia and he gave Ted it too.

In the second parts of these sentences *pneumonia* is not interpreted as being dominant, since it has been mentioned already in the first part. It is claimed that (46b) is unacceptable since the structure of the second part of (46b) forces a dominant interpretation on *it*. However, the question why such constructions as (47) are not allowed remains unexplained.

(47) *John gave pneumonia to Mary.

The examples in (48), raised by Green (1974), also seem to be serious counterexamples for Erteschik-Shir.

(48) a. *Martha gave a piece of her mind to John.
     b. *Martha gave John a piece of her mind,
        and then she gave one to Richard.

In the second part of (48b), *a piece of her mind* pronominalized by the indefinite pronoun *one*, is most likely to be interpreted nondominantly since it has already been mentioned in the first part. Under rule (17), (48b) should be well-formed.

As already mentioned, Dative-shift in English has two criterial features: one is the change in order of two objects and the other is the change in prepositionality. What is common to Erteschik-Shir and Givón is that they take the former as the essential feature of Dative-shift, paying no serious attention to the fact that the prepositional indirect object loses its preposition. Green (1974) takes quite a different position. She argues that the two features are independent of each other and that the crucial feature is the prepositionlessness of the immediately postverbal indirect object, not its position. In support of this view, she compares examples such as (32) and (33) with (49) and (50) by way of demonstrating that the order of constituents is independent of whether or not the verb allows Dative-shift, and points out that discourse structure cannot account for the fact that the prepositional indirect object loses its preposition in (33) but retains it in (49b) and (50b).

(49) a. ?John demonstrated the sixteen proofs for the existence of God which he found in a medieval manuscript over the weekend to me.

b. John demonstrated to me the sixteen proofs for the existence of God which he found in a medieval manuscript over the weekend.

(50) a. ?Arthur will try to obtain the recommendations which you say I need for me.

b. Arthur will try to obtain for me the recommendations which you say I need.

Examples (26)–(29) also cannot be strong evidence for the hypothesis that the primary function of Dative-shift is a discourse function, because the occurrence of it in the leftmost position is not inherent in Dative-shift, as shown in (51).

(51) a. John said these words to Bill.
b. John said to Bill these words.
c. John said to Bill the words he had just learned.
d. John said it to Bill.
e. *John said to Bill it.

There is another problem that the discourse analysis of Dative-shift cannot deal with. The NPs to be shifted are restricted to Goal; Source NPs cannot be shifted.

(52) a. John took away a book from Mary.
b. *John took away Mary a book.
c. *John took Mary away a book.

(53) a. John stole a book from Mary.
    b. *John stole Mary a book.

We have so far argued that the assumption that Dative-shift is merely a discourse function cannot account for its semantically conditioned nature and exceptions.

2.2 Word-order Variation in Japanese and Dative-shift

Givón argues that the main and most common function of dative-shift is that it makes a promoted NP more topical and a demoted NP a focus. This change in topicality is shown in the following test.

(54) a. When he found it, John gave the book to Mary.
    b. ?When he found it, John gave Mary the book.

(55) What did you do to the wall?
    a. I sprayed it with paint.
    b. ?I sprayed paint on it.

(56) What did you do with the paint?
    a. I sprayed it on the wall.
    b. ?I sprayed the wall with it.

He treats the change in case marking that accompanies Dative-shift as a language-specific feature, not an essential one. He therefore claims that the Dative-shift in English has the same function as the word-order variation in SOV languages exemplified in (7) and (8). This kind of word-order variation is also found in Japanese, an SOV language.

(57) a. watasi-ga   John-ni   hon-o   age-ta
        I-Nom   John-Dat   book-Acc   give-Past
        'I gave John a book.'

    b. watasi-ga   hon-o   John-ni   age-ta
        I-Nom   book-Acc   John-Dat   give-Past
        'I gave a book to John.'

This word-order variation is exploited to change the relative topicality of the constituents and assign focus as shown below.

(58) a. watasi-ga   kaban-kara   issatuno hon-o   toridasi,
        I-Nom   bag-Abl   one book-Acc   take-out-and
        sono hon-o   John-ni   age-ta
        the book-Acc   John-Dat   give-Past
        'I took a book out of my bag, and gave the book to John.'

b. ?watasi-ga   kaban-kara   issatuno hon-o   toridasi,
   I-Nom   bag-Abl   one book-Acc   take-out-and,
   John-ni   sono hon-o   age-ta
   John-Dat   the book-Acc   give-Past
   'I took out a book of my bag, and gave to John the book.'

Clearer evidence that word-order variation functions to change the relative topicality of the two NPs comes from the manner in which the two NPs combine with the particle *wa*. Kuno (1973) and Inoue (1983) point out that the particle *wa* indicates either the topic of a sentence when it is assigned to an NP conveying given information, or "contrast" when it is attached to an NP conveying new information.

(59) gakusei-ga   suunin   kega-o   si-ta.
     student-Nom   several   injury-Acc   do-Past
     karera-wa   gakko-ni   tsuita-bakari-dat-ta.
     they-Top   school-Dat   arrive-just-be-Past
     'Several students were injured. They had just arrived at school.'

(60) mise-wa   manin desi-ta-ga,   *roojin-wa*   amari-inakat-ta
     shop-Top   crowded be-Past-but   old-people-Cont   much-not be-Past
     'The shop was crowded, but old people were few
     (though there were many young people).'

Karera 'they', which has been mentioned in the preceding sentence, is interpreted as the topic, while *roojin* 'old person(s)', which has not been mentioned, is interpreted as being a contrastive expression. Compare now the following expressions.

(61) John-ni   ringo-o   age-ta
     John-Dat   apple-Acc   give-Past
     '[I] gave to John an apple.'

  a. John-ni-*wa*   ringo-o   age-ta
     John-Dat   apple-Acc   give-Past

  b. John-ni   ringo-*wa*   age-ta
     John-Dat   apple(Acc)   give-Past

(62) ringo-o   John-ni   ageta
     apple-Acc   John-Dat   give-Past
     '[I] gave an/the apple to John.'

  a. ringo-*wa*   John-ni   age-ta
     apple(Acc)   John-Dat   give-Past

  b. ringo-o   John-ni-*wa*   age-ta
     apple-Acc   John-Dat   give-Past

John in (61a) can be interpreted either as a topic, as in (63a), or as contrastive, as in (63b).

(63) a. A: John-ni   nani-o   age-masi-ta-ka
         John-Dat   what-Acc   give-Honorific-Past-Interrog
         'What did you give to John?'
      B: John-ni-*wa* ringo-o   age-masi-ta
         John-dat   apple-Acc   give-Honorific-Past
         '[I] gave to John an apple.'

   b. John-ni-*wa*   ringo-o   age,
      John-Dat   apple-Acc   give
      Mary-ni-*wa*   nasi-o   age-ta.
      Mary-Dat   pear-Acc   give-Past
      'To John, I gave an apple, and to Mary, I gave a pear.'

Ringo 'apple' in (61b) however, can only be interpreted as contrastive. Sentence (61b) is most likely to be interpreted as '[I] gave John an apple but nothing else'. The same difference exists between (62a) and (62b). Our argument so far shows that the difference in Dative word order is employed to change the relative topicality and focus assignment between two arguments, so that the leftmost constituent is topical and the rightmost constituent is in focus. It follows that, according to Givón's assumption, Dative-shift in English and the similar Japanese word-order variation have the same function, although there is some "trivial" difference in that English shows a change in case-marking while Japanese does not. The word-order variation in Japanese, however, differs drastically from Dative-shift in English in that it has no exception. The word-order variation in Japanese is neither lexically nor semantically conditioned; it is allowed no matter what the verb is or what the semantic contents of the NPs are. For instance, there is no animacy constraint on word-order variation in Japanese, as can be seen in (64).

(64) a. watasi-ga   London-ni   tegami-o   okut-ta.
         I-Nom   London-Dat   letter-Acc   send-Past
         'I sent to London a letter.'

     b. watasi-ga   tegami-o   London-ni   okut-ta.
        I-Nom   letter-Acc   London-Dat   send-Past
        'I send a letter to London.'

From these differences, one can plausibly conclude that the Japanese word-order variation, unlike the Dative-shift in English, is motivated purely by discourse considerations.

Givón treats as Dative-shift not only the alternation between 'give *x* to *y*' and 'give *y x*', but also the alternation between 'spray *x* on *y*' and 'spray *y* with *x*'. As pointed out in relation to (54)–(56), it is claimed that the function is to change the relative topicality and to assign focus. Japanese also has oppositions comparable to that between 'spray *x* on *y*' and spray *y* with *x*'.

(65) a. watasi-ga   mizu-o   baketu-ni   mitasi-ta
        I-Nom   water-Acc   bucket-Dat   fill-Past
        'I filled water into a bucket' (literally).

   b. watasi-ga   mizu-de   baketu-o   mitasi-ta
      I-Nom   water-Instr   bucket-Acc   fill-Past
      'I filled a bucket with water.'

There are changes in case-marking in (65). Recall that the word-order variation in Japanese is exceptionless. The combination of the differentiation in case-marking and the word-order variation produces the following four possibilities, and they are all quite acceptable.

(66) a. watasi-ga   mizu-o   baketu-ni   mitasi-ta
        I-Nom   water-Acc   bucket-Dat   fill-Past
        'I filled water into a bucket.'

   b. watasi-ga   baketu-ni   mizu-o   mitasi-ta
      I-Nom   bucket-Dat   water-Acc   fill-Past
      'I filled into a bucket water.'

   c. watasi-ga   baketu-o   mizu-de   mitasi-ta
      I-Nom   bucket-Acc   water-Instr   fill-Past
      'I filled a bucket with water.'

   d. watasi-ga   mizu-de   baketu-o   mitasi-ta
      I-Nom   water-Instr   bucket-Acc   fill-Past
      'I filled with water a bucket.'

The word-order variation in (66) is purely pragmatic. The more topical constituent takes the leftmost position, while the constituent in focus takes the rightmost position, as verified in (67).

(67) a. watasi-ga   ido-kara   mizu-o   kumi,
        I-Nom   well-from   water-Acc   draw
                     sore-o   *baketu-ni* *mitasi-ta*
        (and)   it-Acc   bucket-Dat   fill-Past
        'I drew water from the well, and filled it into a bucket.'

b.	?watasi-ga	ido-kara	mizu-o	kumi,
	I-Nom	well-from	water-Acc	draw
		baketu-ni	*sore-o*	*mitasi-ta*
	(and)	bucket-Dat	it-Acc	fill-Past

'I drew water from the well, and filled it into a bucket.'

c.	?watasi-ga	ido-kara	mizu-o	kumi,
	I-Nom	well-from	water-Acc	draw
		baketu-o	*sore-de*	*mitasi-ta*
	(and)	bucket-Acc	it-Instr	fill-Past

'I drew water from the well, and filled a bucket with it.'

d.	watasi-ga	ido-kara	mizu-o	kumi,
	I-Nom	well-from	water-Acc	draw
		sore-de	*baketu-o*	*mitasi-ta*
	(and)	it-Instr	bucket-Acc	fill-Past

'I drew water from the well, and filled a bucket with it.'

Sentences (67b) and (67c) are a little unnatural since the topical NP, which has already been mentioned in the first part of the sentence, is placed to the right of the focus NP. It seems very plausible intuitively that sentences (66a) and (66b), which have the same case-marking, are logically about *mizu* 'water' or its change of location. Similarly, (66c) and (66d) are both about *baketu* 'bucket', in spite of the difference in word-order and focus assignment. These observations show that the word-order variation and the case-marking variation in (66) are independent of each other, and the former is a purely pragmatic operation while the latter is a semantic one. Now compare the English sentences in (68) and Japanese ones in (66). It will be noticeable that the possibilities in (66b) and (66d) are blocked in English. The reason for this seems to me quite straightforward. The direct object, which is marked by the accusative postposition in Japanese, is marked in English by the immediately postverbal position without a preposition. This language-specific property in case-marking blocks possibilities (68b) and (68d).

(68) a. I sprayed the paint on the wall.
b. *I sprayed on the wall the paint.
c. I sprayed the wall with the paint.
d. *I sprayed with the paint the wall.

In a language in which possibilities like (68b) and (68d) are blocked, the functions that were otherwise performed by the blocked word-orders are performed by the existing word-orders, producing pragmatic ambiguity.

(69) a. I bought some paint, and sprayed it on the wall.
b. I cleared the wall of pictures, and sprayed paint on it.
c. I bought some paint, and sprayed the wall with it.
d. I cleared the wall of pictures, and sprayed it with paint.

The examples in (69) indicate that in the word-orders 'spray x on y' and 'spray y with x', either x or y can be topical.

The discussion so far clearly demonstrates that the *spray*-type syntactic opposition as in (68a) and (68b) is not pragmatically motivated but semantically motivated. In fact, the *spray*-type opposition seen both in English and Japanese is lexically conditioned, like the *give*-type Dative-shift in English and unlike Japanese word-order variation. It has already been pointed out in the previous chapter that (68a) is, in a logical sense, about the change in location undergone by *the paint*, while (68c) is about the change in condition undergone by *the wall*. Therefore, verbs that express only a change in location cannot have the *spray*-type opposition. The English verb *put* and the Japanese verb *sosogu* 'pour' are typical examples.

(70) a. I put the paint on the wall.
b. *I put the wall with the paint.

(71) a. watasi-wa   baketu-ni   mizu-o   sosoi-da
       I-Top   bucket-Dat   water-Acc   pour-Past
       'I poured water into a bucket.'

   b. *watasi-wa   baketu-o   mizu-de   sosoi-da
       I-Top   bucket-Acc   water-Instr pour-Past
       'I poured a bucket with water.'

Foley and Van Valin (1985) adopt an eclectic position on this issue. They claim that the *give*-type alternation represents "pragmatic dative shift," which involves only a rearrangement of constituents for purely pragmatic reasons, while the *spray*-type alternation represents semantic Dative-shift, which involves an important semantic differentiation. However, this position cannot explain why the *give*-type Dative-shift in English, unlike the purely pragmatic word-order variation in SOV languages, is subject to many lexical and semantic conditions. Stronger evidence against the view that the *give*-type Dative-shift in English is purely pragmatic comes from the study of Korean data in the following section.

2.3 Double-accusative Constructions in Korean

Korean, another SOV language, has purely pragmatically motivated word-order variation.

(72) a. nay-ka   John-eykey   chayk-ul   cwu-essta
       I-Nom   John-Dat   book-Acc   give-Past
       'I gave to John a book.'

     b. nay-ka   chayk-ul   John-eykey   cwu-essta
       I-Nom   book-Acc   John-Dat   give-Past
       'I gave a book to John.'

(73) a. emeni-ka   os-ey   phwul-ul   meki-essta
       mother-Nom   clothes-Dat   starch-Acc   feed-Past
       'Mother added to the clothes some starch/starched the clothes.'

     b. emeni-ka   phwul-ul   os-ey   meki-essta
       mother-Nom   starch-Acc   clothes-Dat   feed-Past
       'Mother added starch to the clothes/starched the clothes.'

These word-order variations in Korean perform the same function as the word-order variation in Japanese, as (74) illustrates.

(74) a. ku-ka   kapang-eyse   hankwen-uy chayk-ul   kkunay-taka,
       he-Nom   bag-from   one-Gen book-Acc   take-out-after
       ku chayk-ul   John-eykey   cwu-essta
       the book-Acc   John-Dat   give-Past
       'He took a book out of his bag, and then gave the book to John.'

(74) b. ?ku-ka   kapang-eyse   hankwen-uy chayk-ul   kkunay-taka,
       he-Nom   bag-from   one-Gen book-Acc   take-out-after
       John-eykey   ku chayk-ul   cwu-essta
       John-Dat   the book-Acc   give-Past
       'He took a book out of his bag, and then gave to John the book.'

The Korean particle *(n)un* has almost the same function as Japanese *wa*. It indicates either the topic of a sentence or "contrast" if it is attached to an NP with given information, while it only expresses contrast if it is attached to an NP with new information. We get exactly the same results for Korean from the test in (75) as we got for Japanese in (61) and (62).

(75) John-eykey   chayk-ul   cwu-essta
     John-Dat   book-Acc   give-Past
     '[I] gave to John a book.'

     a. John-eykey-*nun* chayk-ul   cwu-essta
       John-Dat   book-Acc   give-Past

     b. John-eykey   chayk-*un*   cwu-essta
       John-Dat   book(Acc)   give-Past

    c. chayk-*un*   John-eykey   cwu-essta
        book(Acc)   John-Dat   give-Past

    d. chayk-ul   John-eykey-*nun*   cwu-essta
        book-Acc   John-dat   give-Past

The particle *(n)un* in (75a) and (75c) indicates that the NPs to which it is assigned are either "topical" or "contrastive," while *(n)un* in (75b) and (75d) is interpreted only as expressing contrast. Furthermore, there are no lexical or semantic constraints on this word-order variation. Thus, we can say that the word-order variation in Korean is purely pragmatically motivated, just as in Japanese. Korean, in addition to the word-order variation, also has so-called "double-accusativization." Some dative and genitive NPs are accusativized, resulting in double-accusative constructions.

(76) a. nay-ka   John-eykey   chayk-ul   cwu-essta
      I-Nom   John-Dat   book-Acc   give-Past
      'I gave a book to John.'

     b. nay-ka   John-ul   chayk-ul   cwu-essta
        I-Nom   John-Acc   book-Acc   give-Past
        'I gave John a book.'

(77) a. emeni-ka   ai-eykey   yak-ul   meki-essta
      mother-Nom   child-Dat   medicine-Acc   feed-Past
      'Mother gave medicine to her child.'

     b. emeni-ka   ai-lul   yak-ul   meki-essta
        mother-Nom   child-Acc   medicine-Acc   feed-Past
        'Mother gave her child medicine.'

     a.' emeni-ka   os-ey   phwul-ul   meki-essta
        mother-Nom   clothes-Dat   starch-Acc   feed-Past
        'Mother added some starch to the clothes/starched the clothes.'

     b.' ?emeni-ka   os-ul   phwul-ul   meki-essta
        mother-Nom   clothes-Acc   starch-Acc   feed-Past
        'Mother added the clothes some starch.'

(78) a. nay-ka   John-uy   son-ul   cap-assda
      I-Nom   John-Gen   hand-Acc   grasp-Past
      'I grasped John's hand.'

     b. nay-ka   John-ul   son-ul   cap-assda
        I-Nom   John-Acc   hand-Acc   grasp-Past
        'I grasped John by the hand.'

(79) a. nay-ka   John-uy/eykeyse   ton-ul   ppayas-assda
       I-Nom   John-Gen/Abl   money-Acc   take-away-Past
       'I took away money from John.'

   b. *nay-ka   John-ul   ton-ul   ppayas-assda
      I-Nom   John-Acc   money-Acc   take-away-Past
      'I took away John money.'

Dative-shift in English and double-accusativization in Korean are similar so far as both promote a noncore or nonaccusative NP into the position of a core or accusative NP. Furthermore, Korean double-accusativization manifests the characteristics common to Dative-shift in English. First, it is constrained by animacy. In general, the NP to be accusativized has to be animate, typically human, as shown in (77). Second, NPs with the semantic role Source cannot be accusativized, as shown in (79). Third, double-accusativization, like English Dative-shift, is lexically conditioned. Verbs like *selmyengha* 'explain' and *malha* 'say' cannot have the double-accusative construction, while *kaluchi* 'teach' can.

(80) a. nay-ka   yenge muncang-ul   John-eykey   kaluchi-essa
       I-Nom   English sentence-Acc   John-Dat   teach-Past
       'I taught an English sentence to John.'

   b. nay-ka   yenge muncang-ul   John-ul   kaluchi-essa
      I-Nom   English sentence-Acc   John-Acc   teach-Past
      'I taught John an English sentence.'

(81) a. nay-ka   yenge muncang-ul   John-eykey   selmyengha-essa
       I-Nom   English sentence-Acc   John-Dat   explain-Past
       'I explained an English sentence to John.'

   b. *nay-ka   yenge muncang-ul   John-ul   selmyengha-essa
      I-Nom   English sentence-Acc   John-Acc   explain-Past
      'I explained John an English sentence.'

The evidence presented above shows that the English *give*-type Dative-shift is comparable to double-accusativization in Korean but not to word-order variation in Korean. The claim by Givón (1979, sec. 4.3.3) and Foley and Van Valin (1985:349) that the change in case-marking involved in the *give*-type Dative-shift is restricted to SVO languages is obviously wrong.

Double-accusativization can combine with pragmatic word-order variation, resulting in the following four possibilities.

(82) a. nay-ka   John-eykey   chayk-ul   cwu-essta
       I-Nom   John-Dat   book-Acc   give-Past
       'I gave to John a book.'

b. nay-ka   chayk-ul   John-eykey   cwu-essta
   I-Nom   book-Acc   John-Dat   give-Past
   'I gave a book to John.'

c. nay-ka   John-ul   chayk-ul   cwu-essta
   I-Nom   John-Acc   book-Acc   give-Past
   'I gave John a book.'

d. nay-ka   chayk-ul   John-ul   cwu-essta
   I-Nom   book-Acc   John-Acc   give-Past
   'I gave a book John.'

Again, these four sentences are all acceptable. If the function of double-accusativization were purely pragmatic, namely, to change the relative topicality between the two constituents and the focus assignment, then it would be a totally unnecessary device, since the same effect is already achieved by word-order variation. Korean also has alternations of the *spray*-type. This alternation, combined with the word-order variation, allows the following four possibilities.

(83) a. nay-ka   ppeynkki-lul   pyek-ey   chilha-essta
        I-Nom   paint-Acc   wall-Loc   paint-Past
        'I painted paint on the wall.'

     b. nay-ka   pyek-ey   ppeynkki-lul   chilha-essta
        I-Nom   wall-Loc   paint-Acc   paint-Past
        'I painted on the wall paint.'

     c. nay-ka   pyek-ul   ppeynkki-lo   chilha-essta
        I-Nom   wall-Acc   paint-Instr   paint-Past
        'I painted the wall with paint.'

     d. nay-ka   ppeynkki-lo   pyek-ul   chilha-essta
        I-Nom   paint-Instr   wall-Acc   paint-Past
        'I painted with paint the wall.'

Compare (82) and (83) with (84) and (85).

(84) a. I gave a book to John.
     b. *I gave to John a book.
     c. I gave John a book.
     d. *I gave a book John.

(85) a. I painted white paint on the wall.
     b. *I painted on the wall white paint.
     c. I painted the wall with white paint.
     d. *I painted with white paint the wall.

The reason why the possibilities (84b) and (84d) are blocked seems straightforward. The constraint should be attributed to the property of English that the direct object is marked by its location in the immediately postverbal position without a preposition. The English constraint on the possibilities in (84b) and (84d) appears to have made it difficult to understand that the purely pragmatically motivated change in word order and the semantically motivated change in case-marking are independent of each other. The two mechanisms, which are kept quite separate in Korean, are conflated in English.

3. The Semantics of Dative-shift

In this section, I argue that the Dative-shift in English and Korean are best explained in semantics.

In the previous chapter, three kinds of change were differentiated by three restrictive modifiers: "Positional," "Possessional," and "Conditional."

(86) a. GOposit (x, y, z)
 b. GOposs (x, y, z)
 c. GOcond (x, y, z)

Having refuted the assumption that the *spray*-type syntactic alternation is pragmatically motivated, we now argue that it should be semantics, in the absence of any other plausible candidate, that motivates the alternation. In our analysis, verbs are classified into two types: univalent verbs which have only one set of thematic relations, and ambivalent verbs which have more than one set of thematic relations. It has been assumed that only ambivalent verbs allow the *spray*-type syntactic alternation. For instance, *drain*, being an ambivalent verb, entails not only that some entity undergoes a positional change, but that the entity denoted by the Source NP undergoes a specific conditional change. The syntactic variants shown by *drain* are assigned semantic representations as follows.

(87) a. John drained water from the pool.
 CAUSE (JOHN, GOposit (WATER, THE POOL, z))
 b. John drained the pool of water.
 CAUSE (JOHN, GOcond (THE POOL, u, EMPTY OF WATER))

The syntactic form (87a) emphasizes the positional change to the water, while (87b) emphasizes the conditional change to the pool. These two changes are the two aspects of an integrated whole denoted by the ambivalent verb *drain*. In (87a), the semantic subject is 'water', while in (87b) it is 'the pool'. In either case, the semantic subject is assigned the semantic role Theme by the rest of the sentence.

The analysis just proposed is also applicable to Korean and Japanese. Compare the following Korean sentences.

(88) a. John-i   pakkeyssu-ey   mul-ul   chayu-essta
         John-Nom   bucket-Dat   water-Acc   fill-Past
         'John filled water in a bucket' (literally).

     b. John-i   pakkeyssu-lul mul-lo   chayu-essta
         John-Nom   bucket-Acc   water-Instr   fill-Past
         'John filled a bucket with water.'

(89) a. John-i   pakkeyssu-ey   mul-ul   pu-essta
         John-Nom   bucket-Dat   water-Acc   pour-Past
         'John poured water into a bucket.'

     b. *John-i   pakkeyssu-lul mul-lo   pu-essta
         John-Nom   bucket-Acc   water-Instr   pour-Past
         *'John poured a bucket with water.'

The verb *chayu* 'fill' is an ambivalent verb that denotes a change in the position of an entity and also a concomitant change in the condition of the Goal of the positional change. The ambivalence of the verb *chayu* is represented as follows.

(90) a. CAUSE (w, GOposit (x, y, z))   (Factitive 1)
     b. CAUSE (w, GOcond (z, u, FILLED WITH x))   (Factitive 2)

The syntactic form (88a) emphasizes the positional change (90a), while (88b) emphasizes the conditional change (90b). The verb *pus* 'pour' is a univalent verb that expresses only a positional change to an entity and not denote a conditional change to the Goal. Thus the semantic nature of the verb *pus* 'pour' blocks the syntactic form (89b). The semantic representations for (88a) and (88b) follow.

(91) a. CAUSE (JOHN, GOposit (WATER, y, BUCKET))
     b. CAUSE (JOHN, GOcond (BUCKET, u, FILLED WITH WATER))

The semantic representations in (91) indicate that in (88a) the semantic subject is *mul* 'water' while in (88b) it is *pakkeyssu* 'bucket'. In other words, sentence (88a) is logically about the change to *mul* 'water' while (88b) is about the change undergone by *pakkeyssu* 'bucket'. This logical topicality should be kept distinct from the pragmatic topicality mentioned in Sections 1 and 2. The pragmatic topicality may be changed by word-order variation, but not the logical topicality. Sentence (88a') is still logically about the change affecting the 'water', while (88b′) is about the change affecting the 'bucket'.

(88) a.′ John-i   mul-ul   pakkeyssu-ey   chayu-essta
         John-Nom   water-Acc   bucket-Dat   fill-Past
         'John filled water in a bucket.'

   b.′ John-i   mul-lo   pakkeyssu-lul   chayu-essta
         John-Nom   water-Instr   bucket-Acc   fill-Past
         'John filled a bucket with water.'

3.1 Ambiguity of Change in Possession

In this section, I propose a semantic account of the *give*-type of Dative-shift in English and Korean. Our semantics has to be capable of explaining the following problems.

a. The lexically conditioned property of Dative-shifts in English and Korean.

b. The semantic constraints on Dative-shifts in English and Korean: the animacy constraint and the constraint that blocks the NP with Source role from being shifted.

c. The exceptions to English Dative-shift pointed out in (41)–(45).

Ikegami (1975) points out that a sentence expressing a "change in possession" like (92) allows two interpretations: (92a) and (92b).

(92) John got first prize.
   a. John (y) ← first prize (x)
   b. John (x) → first prize (y)
      (x = what changes, y = Goal of change)

In the first interpretation, what changes is *first prize* and the sentence concerns who its possessor is. In the second interpretation, what undergoes change is *John* and the sentence is about whether or not he possesses the prize. Ikegami says that the former interpretation is related to a "change in locus," and the latter to a "change in condition." I adopt his dual interpretation of a "change in possessorship."

Let us consider a prototypical situation in which a change in possession takes place, such as the situation denoted by a proposition like *John brought Mary a book*. This situation is analyzable into three kinds of changes integrated into one proposition: the positional change of *a book* to *Mary*, a possessional change of *a book* from *John* to *Mary* and a conditional change to *Mary*. The change in possession presupposes the positional change, and the conditional change presupposes the possessional change in this case. These three kinds of changes are represented as follows:

(93) a. GOposit (x, y, z)
  b. GOposs (x, y, z)
  c. GOcond (z, u, WITH x)

Logically, the positional change (93a) does not necessarily entail the possessional change (93b). This is clear from the fact that (94) does not express any change in possession.

(94) John went to the classroom.

Moreover, a change in possession need not entail a change in position, as is clear from (95).

(95) John's property went to his eldest son.

However, a change in possession such as that represented in (93b) always entails the change in condition (93c). When some entity goes into the possession of some person, the person necessarily goes into the condition of possessing it. On the other hand, the conditional change (93c) does not necessarily presuppose a change in possession (93b). One can make somebody possess something without giving it to him, as in (96).

(96). John made Mary make a toy for herself.

In other words, (93b) is a subset of (93c).

(97) GOposs (x, y, z) ⊂ GOcond (z, u, WITH x)

Our assumption is that a language may reflect this "logical inclusion relation" and that Dative-shift is a reflection of the ambiguity of a change in possession. We consider that the alternative syntactic forms shown by the Dative-shift verbs correspond to the thematic role structures (93b) and (93c), as exemplified in (98).

(98) a. John gave a book to Mary.
  a.' CAUSE (JOHN, GOposs (A BOOK, JOHN, MARY))
  b. John gave Mary a book.
  b.' CAUSE (JOHN, GOcond (MARY, u, WITH A BOOK))

(99) a. John-i   Cholsu-eykey   chayk-ul   cwu-essta
     John-Nom   Cholsu-Dat   book-Acc   give-Past
     'John gave a book to Cholsu.'
  a' CAUSE (JOHN, GOposs (A BOOK, JOHN, CHOLSU))
  b. John-i   Cholsu-lul   chayk-ul   cwu-essta
     John-Nom   Cholsu-Acc   book-Acc   give-Past
     'John gave Cholsu a book.'
  b.' CAUSE (JOHN, GOcond (CHOLSU, u, WITH BOOK))

DATIVE-SHIFT: DISCOURSE VS. SEMANTIC APPROACHES

First, our assumption that the thematic role structures of the Dative-shift in English and Korean alternate between a possessional one and a conditional one is compatible with the animacy constraint on the Dative-shift.

(100) a. John brought the piano to New York.
 b. *John brought New York the piano.

(101) a. John brought the piano to Bill.
 b. John brought Bill the piano.

(102) a. John-i   Seoul-ey   phyenci-lul   ssu-essta
       John-Nom   Seoul-Dat   letter-Acc   write-Past
       'John sent a letter to Seoul.'

 b. *John-i   Seoul-lul   phyenci-lul   ssu-essta
       John-Nom   Seoul-Acc   letter-Acc   write-Past
       'John sent Seoul a letter.'

(103) a. John-i   Cholsu-eykey phyenci-lul   ssu-essta
       John-Nom   Cholsu-Dat   letter-Acc   write-Past
       'John sent a letter to Cholsu.'

 b. John-i   Cholsu-lul   phyenci-lul   ssu-essta
       John-Nom   Cholsu-Acc   letter-Acc   write-Past
       'John sent Cholsu a letter.'

As already pointed out, a positional change does not necessarily entail a possessional change. In order for a positional change to entail a possessional change, the Goal has to be an entity that is capable of "possessing," that is, it has to be animate, typically human. This is why (100b) and (102b) are ungrammatical. Sentence (101a) allows two interpretations, represented in (104).

(104) a. CAUSE (JOHN, GOposit (THE PIANO, y, BILL))
 b. CAUSE (JOHN, GOposs (THE PIANO, JOHN, BILL))

The first representation means that John brought the piano to the position of Bill. In this interpretation, *Bill* is only a locative Goal. Dative-shift is possible only in the interpretation (104b).

The second set of data our semantics can account for is sentences in which Dative-shift is obligatory.

(105) a. *Mary gave an inferiority complex to John.
 b. Mary gave John an inferiority complex.

(106) a. *Mary gave a broken arm to John.
 b. Mary gave John a broken arm.

(107) a. *Mary gave a pain in the neck to John.
      b. Mary gave John a pain in the neck.

Green (1974) points out that when *give* means 'provide with' as opposed to 'present as a gift', the indirect object is restricted to a prepositionless form, and the action in many cases can be conceived of as nonvolitional. *Give* in (108) is interpreted in the 'provide with' and nonvolitional sense. When *give* has this sense, it may have an abstract subject, as in (109). On the other hand, *give* in (110) is interpreted only in the 'present as a gift' sense. *Give* with this meaning cannot have an abstract subject.

(108) a. Mary gave John an idea.
      b. Mary gave John the clue to the Sphinx's riddle.

(109) a. Mary's behavior gave John an idea.
      b. Mary's behavior gave John the clue to the Sphinx's riddle.

(110) a. Mary gave an idea to John.
      b. Mary gave the clue to the Sphinx's riddle to John.

(111) a. *Mary's behavior gave an idea to John.
      b. *Mary's behavior gave the clue to the Sphinx's riddle.

A similar problem arises in the following sentences.

(112) a. Greta showed Sam the meaning of true love.
      b. Greta showed the meaning of true love to Sam.

(113) a. The accident showed Sam the meaning of true love.
      b. *The accident showed the meaning of true love to Sam.

(114) a. Several mistakes taught John the secrets of Chinese cooking.
      b. *Several mistakes taught the secrets of Chinese cooking to John.

Sentence (112a) is about the effect of Greta's behavior on Sam, while (112b) reports that Greta pointed out to him some linguistic or philological description for the purpose of having him take it in. Therefore, the subject of (112a) can be replaced by an abstract NP, as in (113a), while such replacement is impossible in (112b), as the ungrammaticality of (113b) shows.

We assumed that Dative-shift involves an alternation between the semantic structures (93b) and (93c). Note that (93a) and (93b) are both about the movement of x to z whether or not the movement is concrete, while (93c) does not express any movement of x. It follows that the most essential function of Dative-shift is to deemphasize, or make abstract, the meaning of movement.

Sentence (105b), (106b), and (107b) do not express any movement on the part of x, whether concrete or abstract. For instance, the situation denoted

DATIVE-SHIFT: DISCOURSE VS. SEMANTIC APPROACHES   49

by (106b) does not include the movement of *a broken arm* from *Mary* to *John*. In (106b), *Mary* is not the Source of a change in possession, and *John* is not the Goal of a possessional change. What (106b) expresses is 'Mary caused John to have a broken arm.' In such cases, prepositional constructions like (106a), which emphasize a possessional change or movement of an entity to a Goal, cannot be used. The so-called "obligatoriness" of Dative-shift in (105)–(107) is a reflection of the logical inclusion relation, namely, that (93b) necessarily entails (93c), but not the other way around.

The data presented in (108)–(111) can be explained along the same lines. The thematic relations of (108a) and (110a) are represented as follows.

   (110a)   Mary gave an idea to John.
            CAUSE (MARY, GOposs (AN IDEA, MARY, JOHN))

   (108a)   Mary gave John an idea.
            CAUSE (MARY, GOcond (JOHN, u, WITH AN IDEA))

Give in (108a) is, as Green pointed out, ambiguous between 'present as a gift' and 'provide with', while *give* in (110a) is conceived of as having only the 'present as a gift' sense. This means that the conditional change to *John* expressed in (108a) may or may not presuppose the possessional change of *an idea* from *Mary* to *John*. This again is quite compatible with our assumption. Logically, (93b) always entails (93c), while (93c) may or may not presuppose (93b). *Give* in (105b), (106b), (107b), (108) and (109) seems to be semantically almost equivalent to *give* as a "causative verb," as in (115).

   (115) They gave me to understand that you would be there.

Give as a causative verb does not necessarily mean the action is volitional. Sentence (115) is most likely to be interpreted as 'they were responsible for the fact that I understood that you would be there'. Sentence (115) also does not report that any change in possession took place. The thematic relations of (115) are represented as in (116), which is basically compatible with (93c).

   (116) CAUSE (THEY, GOcond (I, u, TO UNDERSTAND THAT ...))

The same explanation is applicable to (112)–(114). The prepositional constructions always express volitional action to cause a possessional change of an entity to a Goal, while the prepositionless constructions do not necessarily do so. When it is impossible to presuppose a possessional movement of an entity to a Goal, then a prepositional construction is impossible.

The third question we have to answer is why Dative-shift is impossible with some verbs in both English and Korean.

(117) a. John explained the story to Bill.
 b. *John explained Bill the story.

(118) a. John said these words to Bill.
 b. *John said Bill these words.

(119) a. John transferred some stock to Bill.
 b. *John transferred Bill some stock.

(120) a. nay-ka   yenge muncang-ul   John-eykey   selmyengha-essta
 I-Nom   English sentence-Acc   John-Dat   explain-Past
 'I explained John an English sentence.'

 b. *nay-ka   yenge muncang-ul   John-ul   selmyengha-essta
 I-Nom   English sentence-Acc   John-Acc   explain-Past
 'I explained John an English sentence.'

(121) a. nay-ka   ikes-ul   John-eykey   malha-essta
 I-Nom   this-Acc   John-Dat   say-Past
 'I said this to John.'

 b. *nay-ka   ikes-ul   John-ul   malha-essta
 I-Nom   this-Acc   John-Acc   say-Past
 'I said John this.'

We have regarded Dative-shift as crucially involving a change of condition. Sentences (117a), (118a), (120a), and (121a)—because of the nature of the action in question—cannot be conceived of (or are not normally conceived of) as changing the condition of the Goal. As Gruber (1976:127) said: "*Tell* indicates that what is told is subsequently heard whereas for *say* it is possible not to be understood. Thus one can say something to a wall, but one will never succeed in telling it to anything."

In order for (93b) to entail (93c), the movement of x to z has to be achieved. However, verbs like *say, explain, selmyengha* 'explain' seem not to guarantee achievement of the movement of x to z. Things become clearer if we regard the expressions *give away* and *give out*, noted by Green (1974) and Larson (1988). Larson says that compounding the Dative-shifting verb *give* with a directional adverb particle indicating centrifugal motion results in phrasal verbs that preserve the notion of "beneficiary" from their stem, but intuitively connote only transfer of possession from a Source, and not transfer of possession to a Goal. These verbs also do not guarantee achievement of the movement of x to y, and therefore do not allow Dative-shift.

(122) a. I gave away money to charity.
  b. *I gave away charity money./*I gave charity away money.
  c. I gave out apples to the children.
  d. *I gave out the children apples./*I gave the children out apples.

Transfer in (119) does not necessarily report a positional change of *some stock* to *Bill*. The change expressed in (119a) is surely possessional. Thus our semantics cannot reject (119b). However, the meanings of verbs are changing all the time and verbs formerly not used for Dative-shift may come to be so used. We can quite imagine that (119b) might become acceptable. Indeed, perhaps it already is for some speakers. Sentence (118b), on the other hand, is not needed, since we already have an appropriate way of saying it, using *tell*.

The last question is why Dative-shift in English and double-accusativization in Korean are blocked in Goal-oriented constructions such as (123) and (124).

(123) a. John stole a book from Mary.
  b. *John stole Mary a book.

(124) a. nay-ka   John-uy/egeyse   ton-ul   ppayas-essta
       I-Nom   John-Gen/Abl   money-Acc   take-away-Past
       'I took away money from John.'

  b. *nay-ka   John-ul   ton-ul   ppayas-essta
      I-Nom   John-Acc   money-Acc   take-away-Past
      'I took away John money.'

Ikegami (1981b, 1982) pointed out that, although the Source and the Goal are on an equal footing from a logical point of view, the realization of the Source tends to be more marked than that of the Goal in language. The markedness of Source is exemplified in (125) and (126).

(125) a. John was/went there.
  b. John came from there.

(126) a. Run [to] behind the wall.
  b. Run from behind the wall.

In (126a), *behind the wall* can be Locative or Goal without any marker, whereas *behind the wall* in (126b) must have *from* to be interpreted as Source. The reason for the markedness of Source is obvious from a functional viewpoint. The actual temporal flow where a transfer takes place is always from Source to Goal. It would be plausible, then, to assume that the linguistic expression of transfer or change is strongly constrained so that it reflects this natural information flow. Because of this constraint, the expression of a change is interpreted as a Source–Goal pattern unless it is overtly marked for the reverse interpretation. A Goal-oriented construction, which goes against this flow, tends to require an overt marker for Source. For this reason, *Mary* in *John stole Mary a book* is interpreted as a Goal, and the sentence cannot mean *John stole a book from Mary*.

In this chapter we have argued that the Dative-shift rules in English and Korean are semantic processes.[2] Our semantic analysis provides a satisfactory explanation for the properties of Dative-shifts in English and Korean that cannot be properly accounted for in the discourse analyses of Dative-shift proposed by Givón and Erteshik-Shir. Our analysis does not preclude discourse approaches to Dative-shift. In Korean and Japanese, the purely pragmatic word-order variation and the semantically motivated change in case-marking are kept apart, while they are conflated in English.

Chapter 3
Double-nominative Constructions in Japanese and Korean

1. The Double-nominative Construction in Japanese

1.1 The Topic–Comment Pattern and the Double-nominative

It is often claimed that Japanese is a language in which the topic–comment pattern is predominant. The topic–comment pattern is realized as [NP-*wa* Predicate] in Japanese. The NP marked by *wa* is not necessarily a grammatical subject. The topic marker *wa* can replace various case markers.

(1) a. John-ga   Mary-ni   kono hon-o   age-ta
       John-Nom   Mary-Dat   this book-Acc   give-Past
       'John gave this book to Mary.'

   b. John-wa   Mary-ni   kono hon-o   age-ta
       'Speaking of John, he gave this book to Mary.'

   c. Mary-(ni)-wa   John-ga   kono hon-o   age-ta
       'Speaking of Mary, John gave her this book.'

   d. kono hon-wa   John-ga   Mary-ni   age-ta
       'Speaking of this book, John gave it to Mary.'

The locative case markers, like the nominative, accusative, and dative case markers, can also be replaced by *wa*.

(2) a. Tokyo-ni   yuuzin-ga   takusan iru
       Tokyo-Loc   friend-Nom   many be
       '[I] have many friends in Tokyo.'

   b. Tokyo-(ni)-wa   yuuzin-ga   takusan iru
       'Speaking of Tokyo, [I] have many friends there.'

(3) a. kono heya-de   tabako-ga   sue-nai
       this room-Loc   cigarette-Nom   can-smoke-not
       'One cannot smoke in this room.'

   b. kono heya-(de)-wa   tabako-ga   sue-nai
       'Speaking of this room, one cannot smoke here.'

Mikami (1960) says that the typical Japanese sentence is one which begins with NP-*wa*. In his work, the following sentences, which have the pattern [NP-*wa* NP-*ga* 'Nom' Predicate], are analyzed under one label as "theme (topic)-predicate" sentences.

(4) a. kono class-wa   dansei-ga   yoku dekiru
       this class-Top male-Nom   well able-to-do
       'Speaking of this class, the boys do well [at studies].'

   b. kono class-wa   John-ga   yoku dekiru
      this class-Top John-Nom   well able-to-do
      'Speaking of this class, John does well [at studies].'

(5) a. nihon-wa   dansei-ga   tanmei da
       Japan-Top   male-Nom   short-lived be
       'As for Japan, the male has a short life span.'

   b. nihon-wa   Tokyo-ga   sumi-yoi
      Japan-Top   Tokyo-Nom   easy-to-live
      'As for Japan, Tokyo is comfortable to live in.'

(6) a. Tokyo-wa   zinkoo-ga   ooi
       Tokyo-Top   population-Nom   much
       'Speaking of Tokyo, it has a big population.'

   b. Tokyo-wa   watasi-no otooto-ga   iru
      Tokyo-Top   my younger-brother-Nom be
      'Speaking of Tokyo, my younger brother is there.'

Kuroda (1965) and Kuno (1973) hold that the (a) sentences and (b) sentences in (4)–(6) are syntactically and semantically distinct. They observe that *dansei-ga* 'male-Nom' in (4a) is ambiguous between two interpretations: an "exhaustive-listing" one and a "neutral-description" one. In the former interpretation, (4a) means 'speaking of this class, boys and only boys do well (and the girls do not do well)', while in the latter interpretation it means 'as for this class, the boys do well'. Kuno (1973:64) says that (4a) indicates in its second interpretation that "in some classes boy do well in their studies, and in some other classes they do poorly, and 'this class' can be characterized as a class in which the boys do well. The sentence does not say anything about the girls in the class." On the other hand, (4b) can only receive the exhaustive-listing interpretation. The same distinction can be drawn in (5). Sentence (5a) is ambiguous between exhaustive-listing and neutral description with regard to *dansei-ga* 'male-Nom', while (5b) can receive only the exhaustive-listing interpretation. Kuno (1973) points out that it is only in the neutral description interpretation that the [NP-*wa* NP-*ga*

Predicate] pattern can be converted into the double-nominative construction [NP-*ga* NP-*ga* Predicate].

(4) a.' kono class-ga   dansei-ga   yoku dekiru
       this class-Nom male-Nom   well are-able

   b.' *kono class-ga John-ga   yoku dekiru
       this class-Nom John-Nom   well are-able

(5) a.' nihon-ga   dansei-ga   tanmei da
       Japan-Nom   male-Nom   short-lived are

   b.' *nihon-ga   Tokyo-ga   sumi-yoi
       Japan-Nom   Tokyo-Nom   easy-to-live

(6) a.' Tokyo-ga   zinkoo-ga   ooi
       Tokyo-Nom   population-Nom   much

   b.' *Tokyo-ga   watasi-no otooto-ga   iru
       Tokyo-Nom   my younger-brother-Nom be

In fact, the second nominative NPs in (4a'), (5a'), and (6a') can receive only a neutral-description interpretation. For instance, (4a') means 'it is this class that the boys do well in'. The NP-*wa* + NP-*ga* constructions that cannot be converted into a double-nominative construction, that is, (4b), (5b), and (6b) are considered to be derived from the following sentences via topicalization of the locative NPs.

(7) kono class-de   John-ga   yoku dekiru
    this class-Loc   John-Nom   well able-to-do
    'John does well [at studies] in this class.'

(8) nihon-de   Tokyo-ga   sumi-yoi
    Japan-Loc   Tokyo-Nom   easy-to-live
    'Tokyo is comfortable to live in in Japan.'

(9) Tokyo-ni   watasi-no otooto-ga   iru
    Tokyo-Loc   my younger-brother-Nom   be
    'My brother is in Tokyo.'

The nominative NPs in (7), (8), and (9) can receive the exhaustive-listing interpretation as in (4b), (5b), and (6b).

The observations by Kuroda and Kuno show that, among [NP-*wa* NP-*ga* Predicate] constructions, only those that can have two explicit nominative NPs, that is, two NPs followed by *ga*, are actually double-nominative constructions (or so-called double-subject constructions, to use a more traditional term).

Kuno considers that the double-nominative constructions (or double-subject constructions) are derived by a transformation called "subjectivization." The double-subject constructions (4a′), (5a′), and (6a′) are derived from (10a), (10b), and (10c), respectively, making the leftmost NP-*no* 'NP-Gen' the new subject of the sentence.

(10) a. kono class-no   dansei-ga   yoku dekiru
        this class-Gen   male-Nom   well able-to-do
        'The boys of this class do well.'

     b. nihon-no   dansei-ga   tanmei da
        Japan-Gen   male-Nom   short-lived be
        'Men in Japan have short life spans.'

     c. Tokyo-no   zinkoo-ga   ooi
        Tokyo-Gen   population-Nom   much
        'Population in Tokyo is big.'

Subjectivization is assumed to apply, in principle, only to the leftmost NP-*no* 'NP-Gen'. However, Kuno says that some locative NPs can be "subjectivized."

(11) a. New York-ni   koosoo-kentiku-ga   ooi
        New York-Loc   high-rise-building-Nom   many
        'In New York there are many high-rise buildings.'

     b. New York-ga   koosoo-kentiku-ga   ooi
        New York-Nom   high-rise-buildings-Nom   many

     c. *New York-no   koosoo-kentiku-ga   ooi
        New York-Gen   high-rise-building-Nom   many

(12) a. New York-ni   koosoo-kentiku-ga   takusan aru
        New York-Loc   high-rise-building-Nom   many exist
        'In New York many high-rise buildings exist.'

     b. New York-ga   koosoo-kentiku-ga   takusan aru
        New York-Nom   high-rise-building-Nom   many exist

     c. *New York-no   koosoo-kentiku-ga   takusan aru
        New York-Gen   high-rise-building-Nom   many exist

This exceptional subjectivization of the locative NP-*ni* is restricted to examples involving an existential statement. Kuno assumes that (13b) is ungrammatical since *ni* in (13a) is a directional particle and the example does not involve an existential statement.

(13) a. gakusei-ga   New York-ni   it-ta
       student-Nom   New York-Loc/Dir   go-Past
       'The students went to New York.'

   b. *New York-ga   gakusei-ga   it-ta
       New York-Nom   student-Nom   go-Past

Kuno's syntactic approach to the double-nominative construction in Japanese is inadequate in two respects. First, it does not provide an account of why some NPs with genitive *no* cannot be "subjectivized."

(14) a. zoo-no   hana-ga   nagai
       elephant-Gen   nose-Nom   long
       'The nose of an elephant is long.'

   b. zoo-ga   hana-ga   nagai
       elephant-Nom   nose-Nom   long
       'The elephant—its nose is long.'

(15) a. John-no   enpitu-ga   akai
       John-Gen   pencil-Nom   red
       'John's pencil is red.'

   b. *John-ga   enpitu-ga   akai
       John-Nom   pencil-Nom   red
       'John—his pencil is red.'

The second point is that not all existential sentences can be converted into double-nominative constructions.

(11) a. New York-ni   koosoo-kentiku-ga   ooi
       New York-Loc   high-rise-building-Nom   many
       'In New York there are many high-rise buildings.'

   b. New York-ga   koosoo-kentiku-ga   ooi
       New York-Nom   high-rise-building-Nom   many
       'New York— there are many high-rise buildings there.'

(16) a. Tokyo-ni   watasi-no ie-ga   aru
       Tokyo-Loc   my house-Nom   exist
       'In Tokyo there is my house.'

   b. *Tokyo-ga   watasi-no ie-ga   aru
       Tokyo-Nom   my house-Nom   exist
       'Tokyo—my house exists there.'

1.2 Semantic Analysis of the Double-nominative

Our concern here is to provide a semantic account of the following data.

(17) a. Tokyo-ni   koosoo-kentiku-ga   takusan aru
       Tokyo-Loc   high-rise-building-Nom   many be
       'In Tokyo there are many high-rise buildings.'

   b. Tokyo-ga   koosoo-kentiku-ga   takusan aru
      Tokyo-Nom   high-rise-building-Nom   many be

(18) a. Tokyo-ni   otooto-ga   iru
       Tokyo-Loc   younger-brother-Nom   be
       'My younger brother lives in Tokyo.'

   b. *Tokyo-ga   otooto-ga   iru
       Tokyo-Nom   younger-brother-Nom   be

(19) a. kono heya-ni   mado-ga   ooi
       this room-Loc   window-Nom   many
       'There are many windows in this room.'

   b. kono heya-ga   mado-ga   ooi
      this room-Nom   window-Nom   many

(20) a. kono heya-ni   hon-ga   issatu aru
       this room-Loc   book-Nom   one be
       'There is one book in this room.'

   b. *kono heya-ga   hon-ga   issatu aru
       this room-Nom book-Nom   one be

(21) a. John-ni   otooto-ga   hitori iru
       John-Dat   younger-brother-Nom   one be
       'There is a younger brother to John.'

   b. John-ga   otooto-ga   hitori iru/aru
      John-Nom   younger-brother-Nom   one be

(22) a. Mary-no   me-ga   kirei da
       Mary-Gen   eye-Nom   beautiful be
       'Mary's eyes are beautiful.'

   b. Mary-ga   me-ga   kirei da
      Mary-Nom   eye-Nom   beautiful be

(23) a. John-no   ude-ga   ore-ta
       John-Gen   arm-Nom   break-Past
       'John's arm got broken.'

   b. John-ga   ude-ga   ore-ta
      John-Nom   arm-Nom   break-Past

(24) a. John-no   enpitu-ga   akai
       John-Gen   pencil-Nom   red
       'John's pencil is red.'

   b. *John-ga   enpitu-ga   akai
       John-Nom   pencil-Nom   red

(25) a. John-no   enpitu-ga   ore-ta
       John-Gen   pencil-Nom   break-Past
       'John's pencil got broken.'

   b. *John-ga   enpitu-ga   ore-ta
       John-Nom   pencil-Nom   break-Past

(26) a. John-no   otoosan-ga   kanemoti da
       John-Gen   father-Nom   rich be
       'John's father is rich.'

   b. John-ga   otoosan-ga   kanemoti da
       John-Nom   father-Nom   rich be

(27) a. John-no   otoosan-ga   okot-ta
       John-Gen   father-Nom   get-angry-Past
       'John's father got angry.'

   b. *John-ga   otoosan-ga   okot-ta
       John-Nom   father-Nom   get-angry-Past

The sentences in (17)–(27) can be divided into three groups. The sentences in (17)–(20) are "positional" sentences, the sentences in (21) are "possessional," and the sentences in (22)–(27) are "conditional" sentences expressing a possessional relation between two NPs.

17–20:   Positional sentences

21:      Possessional sentences

22–27:   Conditional sentences with NP-*no* 'Gen' NP

Kitahara (1984) analyzes double-nominative sentences like (22b) and (23b) in terms of the "whole–part" relation. In (28), which is a familiar example in Japanese grammar, he designates the first NP-*ga* the "whole nominative," and the second NP-*ga* the "part nominative."

(28) zoo-ga   hana-ga   nagai
     elephant-Nom nose-Nom   long
     'An elephant—its nose is long.'

He claims that the whole-nominative NP *zoo-ga* does not have any immediate relation with the predicative Adj *nagai*. *Nagai* has an immediate relation with the part-nominative NP *hana-ga*, and the combination of the part-nominative NP and the predicative Adj is related to the whole-nominative NP. His analysis can be illustrated as in (29).

(29) [zoo-ga [hana-ga nagai]]

In his analysis, the combination of the part-nominative and its predicate functions as the predicate for the whole-nominative NP. In fact, some double-nominative constructions can be paraphrased into single-nominative constructions with a compound predicate in which the part-nominative NP is incorporated.

(30) a. John-ga   asi-ga   mizikai
       John-Nom   leg-Nom   short
       'John—his legs are short.'

   b. John-ga   tansoku da
      John-Nom   short-legged be
      'John is short-legged.'

(31) a. Mary-ga   iro-ga   kuroi
       Mary-Nom   color-Nom   black
       'Mary—her color is dark/Mary has a dark complexion.'

   b. Mary-ga   iro-guro-da
      Mary-Nom   color-blacked
      'Mary is dark-complexioned.'

A similar analysis was proposed by Izui (1970). He calls the double-nominative construction a "ditopical expression."

> Under the term of "ditopical," I mean a syntactic construction where two subjects in Nominative case (or two topics) function together in a single sentence, and the first of the two is the major subject and, as the indicator of the general theme of the whole sentence, is generally put at the head of the sentence. The second may be called the minor subject and is in closer connection with the predicate than the major subject is. (Izui 1970:427)

He considers that since the sequence of the second nominative NP and the predicate functions in its entirety as the predicate to the first nominative NP, the meaning of the sentence is to be understood as in (32).

(32) NP_1 is such that NP_2 ...

Sentence (28), in Izui's view, means something like 'an elephant is such an animal that its nose is long'.

The analyses by Kitahara and Izui suggest that the double-nominative sentence (28) is a statement about the nature or attributes of an elephant, while (33) is about the nature or attributes of an elephant's nose.

(33) zoo-no   hana-ga   nagai
      elephant-Gen   nose-Nom   long
      'The nose of an elephant is long.'

The semantic structure of (33) and (28) can be represented as in (34) and (35).

(34) BEcond (THE NOSE OF ELEPHANT, LONG)

(35) BEcond (AN ELEPHANT, y)
      y = BEcond (NOSE, LONG)
      → BEcond (AN ELEPHANT, WITH A LONG NOSE)

These representations say that the semantic subject of (33) is *zoo-no hana* 'the nose of an elephant' and is assigned the semantic role Theme, while the semantic subject and the Theme of (28) is *zoo* 'elephant'. Thus the syntactic alternation between (33) and (28), which was characterized by Kuno as involving a "subjectivization transformation," is redefined as a syntactic alternation reflecting an alternation of thematic relations. Our primary concern now is whether logical inference based on "logical inclusion relations" has predictive power in the analysis of the double-nominative construction, as it did in the study of the Dative-shifts of English and Korean. We have differentiated three kinds of 'change', indicated by GO in (36), and assumed that the possibility of Dative-shift in English and Korean reflects the logical inclusion relations holding between (36a), (36b), and (36c).

(36) a. GOposit (x, y, z)
      b. GOposs (x, y, z)
      c. GOcond $(z, u,$ WITH $x)$ or GOcond $(y, u,$ WITHOUT $x)$

We now posit three parallel kinds of 'state', indicated by BE in (37a), (37b), (37c), and hypothesize that the possibility of conversion into the double-nominative construction reflects the logical inclusion relations obtaining among them.

(37) a. BEposit (x, y)
      b. BEposs (x, y)
      c. BEcond $(y,$ WITH $x)$

As we assumed that the double-nominative construction is about an attribute of, or the identity of, the semantic subject realized as the first nominative

NP of the sentence, it must be represented by (37c). Therefore, what is relevant here is the logical inclusion relation between (37a) and (37c), and between (37b) and (37c). Obviously, (37b) always entails (37c). When an entity x is in the possession of y, y is necessarily in the condition of possessing x. However, (37a) does not necessarily entail either (37b) or (37c). For instance, it is hard to suppose that either the *station* or the *department store* undergoes any change in condition in consequence of the positional change of John in (38).

(38) John went to the station from the department store.

Similarly, it is hard in normal circumstances to claim that in (39) John's location in the department store gives some property or condition to the department store.

(39) John is in the department store.

In order for (36a) and (37a) to entail (36c) and (37c), respectively, there must be an extra condition. In the case of Dative-shift, this extra condition is the ambivalence of verbs. Alternation of the thematic relations from (36a) to (36c) is blocked unless the verb contains in its semantic content the Goal or the Source of a conditional change.

(40) a. John put a book on the table.
          CAUSE (JOHN, GOposit (A BOOK, y, ON THE TABLE))
      b. *John put the table with a book.

(41) a. John drained water from the pool.
          CAUSE (JOHN, GOposit (WATER, THE POOL, z))
      b. John drained the pool of water.
          CAUSE (JOHN, GOcond (THE POOL, u, EMPTY OF WATER))

The verb *drain*, unlike *put*, contains in its semantic content the Goal of a conditional change which can be represented as something like EMPTY OF x. This ambivalence of *drain*, as an extra condition, facilitates the entailment of (36c) from (36a).

Let us consider the possessional sentence (21a). As already pointed out, BEposs in (37b) necessarily entails BEcond in (37c). A state expressed by (37b) is the abstract location of x, the thing possessed. In other words, (37b) expresses 'where x is', 'in whose possession x lies'. In this sense (37b) is closely related to the positional location of x expressed in (37a). Our assumption is that the syntactic forms (21a) and (21b) correspond to (37b) and (37c), respectively. The assumption that (21a) corresponds to (37b) is reinforced by the fact that the same verb and the same case markers are used both in the positional sentence (20a) and the possessional sentence (21a).

Sentence (20a) is about the concrete location of *hon* 'book', marked by the nominative postposition *ga*, in *heya* 'room' marked by the dative-locative postposition *ni*. Similarly, (21a) is semantically about the abstract location of *otooto* 'younger brother', marked by *ga*, in relation to John, marked by *ni*. Thus the semantic structure of (21a) can be represented as in (42).

(42) BEposs (A YOUNGER BROTHER, JOHN)

The double-nominative sentence (21b) is semantically about *John*, which constitutes the subject of the whole sentence, that is, the semantic subject. The thematic relations expressed in (21b) may be represented as follows.

(43) BEcond (JOHN, WITH A YOUNGER BROTHER)

Our analysis predicts that every possessional sentence like (21a) can be converted into a double-nominative sentence because (37b) necessarily entails (37c). This prediction seems to be correct. I cannot find any exception to the syntactic alternation between a possessional sentence with the NP-*ni* + NP-*ga* pattern and a double-nominative sentence.

(44) a. John-ni   okane-ga   takusan aru
          John-Dat   money-Nom   much be
          'There is a lot of money to John.'

     b. BEposs (A LOT OF MONEY, JOHN)

(45) a. John-ga   okane-ga   takusan aru
          John-Nom   money-Nom   much be

     b. BEcond (JOHN, WITH A LOT OF MONEY)

The analysis proposed above incorporates the claim that the double-nominativization of a possessional sentence is a process comparable to that of Dative-shift in English and Korean: the former applying to static situations and the latter to dynamic situations.

We now turn to the positional sentences in (17)–(22). The positional existence of x in y does not necessarily entail that y is in a specific condition owing to the existence of x. It follows that the conversion of a positional sentence into a double-nominative sentence tends to be blocked. Our assumption is that (37a) entails (37c) only when it is easily recognized that the existence of x in y, because of the nature of x, attributes some property or condition to y. Compare (17) and (18). The existence of a lot of high-rise buildings in it can easily be recognized as one likely property of a city.

Sentence (17b) means 'Tokyo is such a city that there are a lot of high-rise buildings in it'. The thematic relations expressed in (17b) can be represented as follows:

(46) BEcond (TOKYO, WITH A LOT OF HIGH-RISE BUILDINGS)

On the other hand, the existence of someone's brother in it can hardly be recognized as a legitimate property of a city. In English one can say (47a), but not (47b).

(47) a. Tokyo has a lot of high-rise buildings.
b. *Tokyo has John's brother.

The same explanation is applicable to (19) and (20).

(48) a. This room has many windows.
b. *This room has one book.

The possibility of converting an existential sentence into a double-nominative sentence seems to be closely connected to the notion of "inalienability," which plays an important role in the third group. Compare (20) and (49).

(49) a. kono heya-ni   mado-ga   hitotu aru
this room-Loc   window-Nom   one exist
'There is one window in this room.'

b. kono heya-ga   mado-ga   hitotu aru
this room-Nom   window-Nom   one exist

Notice, too, that the English sentence (50) seems acceptable, unlike (48b).

(50) This room has one window.

What makes (49b) acceptable, in contrast to (20b), is that a window can be in an inalienable relation to a room, whereas a book cannot. Admittedly there is no clear-cut distinction between "alienable" and "inalienable." The crucial thing is that the existence of a window in a room attributes a property to the room, whereas the existence of a book does not. A window and a book differ in kind, or in quality. Comparison of the unacceptable (20b) with the acceptable (51) suggests that quantity may compensate for quality. In other words, while the presence of one book in a room may not characterize the room, the presence of many books may.

(51) kono heya-ga   hon-ga   takusan aru
this room-Nom   book-Nom   many exist
'This room—there are many books here.'

We turn now to the third group. Generally, the condition or property of an entity possessed by or related to someone does not necessarily characterize the possessor. Nor is it the case that when the entity possessed by or related to someone is affected, the possessor is necessarily affected. The semantic structures of (24a) and (25a) are represented as (52) and (53) respectively.

(52) BEcond (JOHN'S PENCIL, RED)

(53) GOcond (JOHN'S PENCIL, *y*, BROKEN)

The semantic representations (52) and (53) do not necessarily entail any specific condition or change in the condition of *John*. It is not natural to say that 'John is such a person whose pencil is red', or 'John is such a person whose pencil was broken'. However, if the possessive relation between two entities is inalienable, or whole–part, the condition or change in condition of the part necessarily entails a condition or change in condition of the whole. There is a necessary entailment between (a) and (b) in (54) and (55), which are the semantic representations for (22) and (23), respectively.

(54) a. BEcond (MARY'S EYES, BEAUTIFUL)
     b. BEcond (MARY, WITH BEAUTIFUL EYES)

(55) a. GOcond (JOHN'S ARM, *y*, BROKEN)
     b. GOcond (JOHN, *u*, WITH A BROKEN ARM)

As pointed out above, the double-nominative construction is allowed when the two entities are in such a relation that a property of one entity attributes a specific property or condition to the other. Compare (26b) ad (56).

(56) *John-ga   ringin-ga   kanemoti da
      John-Nom   neighbor-Nom   rich be

Having a rich father involves being in a particular condition, but having a rich neighbor does not. Similarly, a sentence expressing a temporary condition cannot be converted into a double-nominative sentence, as (27) shows. One cannot say that 'John is such a person whose father got angry'.

The discussion so far shows that the double-nominative construction is allowed only when one NP's condition or change of condition entails a condition or change of condition in the subject NP of the sentence.

1.3 Syntactic Description

The discussion in the previous section suggests that, in (57), the second nominative NP plus the predicate (Pred) function together as a predication about the first nominative construction.

(57) [NP-*ga*] [NP-*ga* Pred]

Our concern in this section is to decide on a syntactic label for the combination of the second nominative NP and the predicate in (57). There are two plausible candidates: one is to consider the combination as an embedded sentence, and the other is to regard it as a compound predicate.

(58) a. [s NP-*ga* [s NP-*ga* V/Adj]]
 b. [s NP-*ga* [V/Adj NP-*ga* V/Adj]]

Teramura (1982) points out that in Japanese there are two kinds of NP + Pred combinations. In one, the combination is so idiomatic that it functions as a compound predicate. In the other, the NP and its predicate do not constitute an idiom. The two types are exemplified in (59) and (60).

(59) *Idiomatic*
 a. hara-ga   tatu
    belly-Nom stand
    'get angry'

 b. ki-ni   iru
    mind-Dat   enter
    'be pleased with'

(60) *Nonidiomatic*
 a. hana-ga   nagai
    nose-Nom   long
    'the nose is long'

 b. me-ga   kirei
    eye-Nom   beautiful
    'eyes are beautiful'

Both kinds of NP + Pred combinations can function as predicates of a larger sentence, as in (61a) and (61b).

(61) a. John-ga   hara-ga   tat-ta
       John-Nom   belly-Nom   stand-Past
       'John got angry.'

 b. John-ga   me-ga   kirei da
    John-Nom   eye-Nom   beautiful be
    'John—his eyes are beautiful.'

The distinction between (61a) and (61b) is demonstrated by syntactic tests. The first test is whether one can ask a question like NP-*ga doo da?* 'How is NP?' or NP-*ga doo sita?* 'What happened to NP?'

(62) a. ??hara-ga   doo si-ta   ——   tat-ta
       belly-Nom how do-Past   stand-Past
       'What happened to the belly?'   'It stood.'

   b. hana-ga   doo da   ——   nagai
      nose-Nom   how be   long
      'How is the nose?'   'It is long.'

The second test is to see whether the transformation from NP + Pred into Adj + NP is possible.

(63) a. hara-ga   tatu   →   *tatu hara
       belly-Nom   stand   standing belly
       'get angry'

   b. ki-ni   iru   →   *iru ki
      mind-Dat   enter   entering mind
      'be pleased with'

   c. hana-ga   nagai   →   nagai hana
      nose-Nom   long   long nose
      'The nose is long.'   'long nose'

   d. me-ga   kirei   →   kirei-na me
      eye-Nom   beautiful   beautiful eye
      'The eyes are beautiful.'   'beautiful eyes'

The results of these tests suggest that the syntactic structure of the double-nominative construction in Japanese is (58a), except in cases where an idiomatic expression like (59a) is used, as in (61a). Further important evidence for choosing (58a) is the fact that, when the combination is not idiomatic, a construction with more than two nominative NPs is possible, as in (64).

(64) Mary-ga   me-ga   hitomi-ga   iro-ga   kirei da
     Mary-Nom eye-Nom   pupil-Nom   color-Nom   beautiful be
     'Mary—her eyes—their pupils—their color is beautiful.'

We may conclude that the syntactic structure of the double-nominative construction in Japanese is as in (65).

(65) [S_1 NP-*ga* [S_2 NP-*ga* ... [S_n NP-*ga* Adj/V]]]

1.4 Conclusion: The Double-nominative in Japanese

1. The syntactic alternation between [NP-*ni* NP-*ga* Pred] or [NP-*no* NP-*ga* Pred] and the double-nominative construction involves an alternation in the semantic structure.

a. BEposit (x, y) → a.′ BEcond $(y, \text{WITH } x)$
b. BEposs (x, y) → b.′ BEcond $(y, \text{WITH } x)$
c. BEcond $(x\text{'s}, z, y)$ → c.′ BEcond (x, u)
   $(u = \text{BEcond}(z, y))$

2. The possibilities of conversion into a double-nominative construction reflect the logical inclusion relations holding between (a) and (a′), (b) and (b′), and (c) and (c′). Formula (b) necessarily entails (b′). This is reflected in the fact that every possessional sentence with the NP-*ni* + NP-*ga* pattern can be converted, without exception, into a double-nominative sentence. This process is comparable to the Dative-shifts of English and Korean. Formulas (a) and (c) do not necessarily entail (a′) and (c′) respectively. Therefore, a sentence with semantic structures (a) and (c) can be converted into a double-nominative sentence only when the condition or change of condition denoted by the combination of an NP and predicate, assisted by an extra condition, can attribute some property or condition to the subject NP of the whole sentence. This extra condition is either an inalienable relation between x and y, or 'largeness in quantity of x' in the alternation between (a) and (a′). Formula (c) can entail (c′) only if x and z are in an inalienable relation, or in a relation that is normally regarded as being inalienable.

3. The syntactic structure of the double-nominative sentence is as follows:

[s_1 NP-*ga* [s_2 NP-*ga* ... [s_n NP-*ga* Adj/V]]]

2. Double-nominative Constructions in Korean

Korean has the same types of double-nominative construction as Japanese.

(66) a. Seoul-ey   kochung-kenmul-i   manhta
        Seoul-Loc   high-rise-building-Nom many
        'In Seoul there are many high-rise buildings.'

     b. Seoul-i   kochung-kenmul-i   manhta
        Seoul-Nom   high-rise-building-Nom many
        'Seoul-many high-rise buildings are there.'

(67) a. Seoul-ey   tongsayng-i   issta
        Seoul-Loc   younger-brother-Nom   be
        'My younger brother lives in Seoul.'

DOUBLE-NOMINATIVE CONSTRUCTIONS 69

    b. *Seoul-i   tongsayng-i   issta
       Seoul-Nom younger-brother-Nom be
       'Seoul-my younger brother lives there.'

(68) a. i pang-ey   changmun-i manhta
       this room-Loc window-Nom are-many
       'There are many windows in this room.'

    b. i pang-i   changmun-i manhta
       this room-Nom window-Nom are-many
       'This room-many windows are there.'

(69) a. i pang-ey   chayk-i   hankwen issta
       this room-Loc book-Nom   one be
       'There is one book in this room.'

    b. *i pang-i   chayk-i   hankwen issta
       this room-Nom book-Nom   one be
       'This room-one book is there.'

(70) a. John-eykey   tongsayng-i   hana issta
       John-Dat   younger-brother-Nom one be
       'There is one younger brother to John.'

    b. John-i   tongsayng-i   hana issta
       John-Nom   younger-brother-Nom one be
       'John-there is one younger brother to him.'

(71) a. Mary-uy   nwun-i   kopta
       Mary-Gen   eye-Nom   beautiful
       'Mary's eyes are beautiful.'

    b. Mary-ka   nwun-i   kopta
       Mary-Nom   eye-Nom   beautiful
       'Mary-her eyes are beautiful.'

(72) a. John-i   phal-i   pule-ci-essta
       John-Gen   arm-Nom   get-broken-Past
       'John's arm got broken.'

    b. John-i   phal-i   pule-ci-essta
       John-Nom   arm-Nom   get-broken-Past
       'John-his arm got broken.'

(73) a. John-uy   yenphil-i   pulkta
       John-Gen   pencil-Nom red
       'John's pencil is red.'

b. *John-i   yenphil-i   pulkta
      John-Nom   pencil-Nom   red
      'John-his pencil is red.'

(74) a. John-uy   yenphil-i   kkekk-ki-essta
      John-Gen   pencil-Nom   get-broken-Past
      'John's pencil got broken.'

   b. *John-i   yenphil-i   kkekk-ki-essta
      John-Nom   pencil-Nom   get-broken-Past
      'John-his pencil got broken.'

(75) a. John-uy   apeci-ka   puca ita
      John-Gen   father-Nom   rich be
      'John's father is rich.'

   b. John-i   apeci-ka   puca ita
      John-Nom   father-Nom   rich be
      'John-his father is rich.'

The positional sentences (66a), (67a), (68a), and (69a) have the semantic structure represented as BEposit (x, y). The existence of x in y does not necessarily attribute a property or a specific condition to y. The existence of x can give a property to y only when it is in an inalienable relation to y, or large in quantity. Sentences (67a) and (69a), which satisfy neither of the two conditions, cannot be converted into a double-nominative construction. It is also the case in Korean, as in Japanese, that a possessional sentence with the NP-Dat + NP-Nom pattern can be converted into a double-nominative construction without exception. This is considered a reflection of the fact that BEposs (x, y) necessarily entails 'BEcond $(y,$ WITH $x)$'. A semantic structure represented as 'BEcond $(x$'s $z, y)$' can attribute a property to y in the case in which z is in an inalienable relation to x. Sentences (73b) and (74b), which do not satisfy this condition, are not acceptable. Double-nominativization is also allowed when z is in a relation with x that is socially regarded as being inalienable, as in (75).

A multiple-nominative construction is also possible in Korean.

(76) Mary-ka   nwun-i   nwuntongca-ka   sayk-i   kopta
     Mary-Nom   eye-Nom   pupil-Nom   color-Nom   beautiful
     'Mary—her eyes—their pupils—their color is beautiful.'

This suggests that the Korean double-nominative construction would be give a syntactic analysis parallel to that in (65).

The foregoing discussion shows that the double-nominative constructions in (66)–(75) are syntactically and semantically identical with Japanese double-nominative constructions.

2.1 Some Differences between Korean and Japanese

Korean has another type of double-nominative construction that is lacking in Japanese.

Korean

(77) John-i   sensayng-i   toy-essta
     John-Nom   teacher-Nom   become-Past
     'John became a teacher.'

Japanese

(78) a. John-ga   sensei-ni   nat-ta
         John-Nom   teacher-Dat   become-Past
         'John became a teacher.'

    a.' *John-ga   sensei-ga   nat-ta
         John-Nom   teacher-Nom   become-Past

The double-nominative construction in (77) is syntactically different from those in (66)–(75) in two respects. First, the double-nominative constructions in (66)–(75), which are assumed to have the syntactic structure (79), allow multiple-nominative constructions in which subsequent NPs further specify the immediately preceding NP.

(79)   [$_{S1}$ NP-Nom [$_{S2}$ NP-Nom ... [$_{Sn}$ NP-Nom Adj/V]]]

However, sentences like (77) do not allow this kind of syntactic expansion. Second, they differ in relation to the omissibility of the nominative postposition. In the first type of double-nominative construction the first nominative postposition is omissible while, in the second type, the second nominative marker is omissible.

(80) a. Mary-ka   nwun-i   kopta
         Mary-Nom   eye-Nom   beautiful
         'Mary-her eyes are beautiful.'

    b. Mary   nwun-i   kopta

    c. *Mary-ka   nwun   kopta

(81) a. John-i   sensayng-i   toy-essta
         John-Nom   teacher-Nom   become-Past
         'John became a teacher.'

    b. *John   sensayng-i   toy-essta

    c. John-i   sensayng   toy-essta

I will call the first type the "A-type" and the second type the "B-type." We shall consider this issue in more detail shortly.

2.2 Japanese naru and Korean toy

Japanese *naru* and Korean *toy*, like English *become*, are the typical verbs for designating a change of condition. The two verbs show different syntactic behavior. First, as already indicated, Korean *toy* can take the double-nominative construction, while Japanese *naru* can only take the nominative–dative pattern.

Japanese

(82) a. kisetu-ga   haru-ni   nat-ta
           season-Nom spring-Dat become-Past
           'The season became spring.'

      b. doo-ga   kin-ni   nat-ta
           copper-Nom gold-Dat   become-Past
           'The copper became gold.'

      c. mizu-ga   koori-ni   nat-ta
           water-Nom   ice-Dat   become-Past
           'The water became ice.'

Korean

(83) a. kyeycel-i   pom-i   toy-essta
           season-Nom spring-Nom become-Past
           'The season became spring.'

      b. tong-i   kum-i   toy-essta
           copper-Nom gold-Nom become-Past
           'The copper became gold.'

      c. mul-i   elum-i   toy-essta
           water-Nom   ice-Nom   become-Past
           'The water became ice.'

Second, *naru* cannot be used as a one-place predicate, while *toy* can.

Japanese

(84) a. haru-ni   nat-ta
           spring-Dat become-Past
           'It became spring.'

b. *kin-ni   nat-ta
   gold-Dat   become-Past

c. *koori-ni   nat-ta
   ice-Dat   become-Past

Korean

(85) a. pom-i   toy-essta
        spring-Nom   become-Past
        'Spring has come.'

   b. kum-i   toy-essta
      gold-Nom   become-Past
      'Gold was made.'

   c. elum-i   toy-essta
      ice-Nom   become-Past
      'Ice was made.'

   d. siksa-cwunpi-ka   toy-essta
      meal-preparation-Nom   become-Past
      'Preparation for a meal was made.'

The Japanese sentence (84a) is often used as an idiomatic expression without a nominative NP. However, it is still interpreted as meaning that 'something turned into spring'. It follows that Japanese *naru* is a two-place predicate that obligatorily requires a nominative NP and a dative NP. The dative postposition *ni* is also typically used as a locative or goal marker, as in (86).

(86) a. John-ga   gakkoo-ni   it-ta
        John-Nom   school-Dat   go-Past
        'John went to school.'

Therefore, the thematic relations of a sentence with *naru* are represented as GO (x, y, z). The semantic structure of (82a), for instance, is represented as (87).

(87) GOcond (SEASON, y, SPRING)

At the same time, the data in (85) indicate that Korean *toy* is a one-place predicate. One might suppose that *toy* is a two-place predicate, claiming that (85a–c) are obtained by deleting the first nominative NP of (83a–c). However, this claim does not hold, since sentence (85b) cannot take another nominative NP. The meaning of *toy* seems to be paraphrasable as something like 'is completed' or 'comes to exist', and the semantic structure of sentences containing *toy* can be represented as GOcond (x, y, EXIST). The semantic structures of (85a–d) are represented in (88a–d) respectively.

(88) a. GOcond (SPRING, y, EXIST)
      b. GOcond (GOLD, y, EXIST)
      c. GOcond (ICE, y, EXIST)
      d. GOcond (PREPARATION FOR MEAL, y, EXIST)

Note that *haru* 'spring' in the Japanese sentence (84a) expresses a passing state of the season. The season passes from winter to spring and from spring to summer. Sentence (84a) can be paraphrased as 'the season passes into the state of spring'. However, *pom* 'spring' in (85a) does not denote a temporal state that the season passes into and out of. The verb *toy* in (85a) does not require 'season' as an argument. What is denoted by *pom* in (85a) is considered to be an independent or self-completing condition. Sentence (85a) can thus be paraphrased as 'the condition of spring came to exist or started existing'.

Ikegami (1981a) points out that there are three possible ways in which languages express change. The first possibility is to extract an entity x that is considered to keep its identity throughout the change. Thus, the change is analyzed as one undergone by x from $-y$ to $+y$, which Ikegami formalizes along the lines of (89).

(89) x GO FROM $-y$ TO $+y$

The second possibility is that, although an entity x is assumed to keep its identity, the change is not a change on the part of x from $-y$ to $+y$, but a change in state from 'x is (in) $-y$' to 'x is (in) $+y$', as represented in (90).

(90) (x WITHOUT y)   GO TO   (x WITH y);
      FROM   (x WITHOUT y)   COME   (x WITH y)

The third possibility is not to posit an entity that keeps its identity through the change, but to understand the change as one from $-y$ to $+y$.

(91) $-y$ GO TO $+y$;
      FROM $-y$ COME $+y$

Ikegami argues that a positional change is typically represented as in (89). *John* in *John went from his house to the station* keeps his identity throughout his movement from *his house* to *the station*. Ikegami also points out that a change in possession can be understood either as (89) or (90). We have already pointed out in the previous chapter that the Dative-shift in English and Korean involves a semantic alternation between (89) and (90). Ikegami says that a change in condition is typically represented as in (91). To posit an entity that keeps its identity is not very significant in analyzing the meanings of the following sentences.

(92) a. Spring became summer.
b. Copper became gold.
c. The pumpkin turned into a handsome young man.

What is important is that Japanese expresses a conditional change not by the logically appropriate formula in (91), but by analogy with a positional change, formalized in (89). The semantic structures of (82a–c) are represented as (93a–c), respectively.

(93) a. GOcond (SEASON, y, SPRING)
b. GOcond (COPPER, y, GOLD)
c. GOcond (WATER, y, ICE)

It seems to be very important in the contrastive study of the two languages to recognize that the verbs they most typically use to express a change of condition differ drastically from each other in the manner in which they express that change. It is worthwhile noting that in old Japanese the verb *naru* had two meanings: 'come into existence' and 'change from one thing into another'. These two meanings are exemplified in (94a) and (94b), respectively, which are quoted from the *Nihon-shoki*, a Japanese classic written in A.D. 720.

(94) a. oya nasi-ni   nanzi   nare-kem-eya
       parent without   thou   had-be-born-Interrog
       'Would you have been born without parents?'

   b. aoyagi-wa   kazura-ni   ... nari-karazu-ya
      willow-Top   creepers-Dat ... become-has-not
      'The willows did not become creepers ...'

Naru in the first meaning is semantically almost identical with Korean *toy*. *Naru* must have gradually lost this meaning, with the result that the second meaning became its basic sense. The usage of *naru* exemplified in (94a) remains only in certain idiomatic expressions like (95).

(95) mi-ga   naru
     fruit/nut-Nom   become
     'Fruits are born.'

The verb comparable to Korean *toy* in present-day Japanese is *dekiru*, which literally means 'come out into existence'.

(96) koori-ga   deki-ta
      ice-Nom   be-made-Past
      'Ice was made/ready.'

Sentence (96) shows that Japanese *dekiru*, like Korean *toy*, is a verb whose meaning can be represented by (91). However, Japanese *dekiru* differs from *toy* in that it cannot have as its subject an NP denoting a condition.

(97) *haru-ga   deki-ta
       spring-Nom   be-made-Past
      'Spring has come.'

Dekiru also cannot take the double-nominative construction.

(98) a. *kisetu-ga   haru-ga   dekiru
         season-Nom   spring-Nom   be-made
     b. *mizu-ga   koori-ga   deki-ta
         water-Nom   ice-Nom   be-made-Past

The problem we now face is how to analyze the B-type double-nominative constructions taken by *toy*, such as (83a) and (81a) which are repeated here as (99a) and (99b).

(99) a. kyeycel-i   pom-i   toy-essta
        season-Nom   spring-Nom   become-Past
        'The season became spring.'

     b. John-i   sensayng-i   toy-essta
        John-Nom   teacher-Nom   become-Past
        'John became a teacher.'

Let us consider the following English sentences.

(100) a. The egg   hatched   into a little chick.
          Theme   Goal

      b. A little chick hatched   from the egg.
          Theme   Source

In the actual situation denoted by these two sentences, it is difficult to consider that *the egg* in (100a) and *a little chick* in (100b) keep their identity through the change. However, English, like Japanese, has a tendency to express conditional change by analogy with positional change. Let us apply the two patterns in (100) to (99b). The first possibility is, following (100a), to assign Theme to the first nominative NP and Goal to the second nominative NP.

(99) b.' John-i   sensayng-i   toy-essta
        Theme   Goal

The verb *toy*, in addition to the double-nominative construction, can take a syntactic structure comparable to that taken by the Japanese *naru* 'become'. The postposition *(u)lo* in the following examples is traditionally called the postposition for the "case of direction," which is similar to English *to*.

(101) a. hopak-i   salam-ulo   toy-essta
         pumpkin-Nom man-to   become-Past
         'The pumpkin turned into a man.'

      b. tong-i   kum-ulo   toy-essta
         copper-Nom   gold-to   become-Past
         'The copper turned into gold.'

      c. ?elum-i   mul-lo   toy-essta
         ice-Nom   water-to   become-Past
         'The ice became water.'

      d. *John-i   sensayng-ulo toy-essta
         John-Nom   teacher-to   become-Past
         'John turned into a teacher.'

The examples in (101) suggest that in Korean the semantic pattern in (100a), unlike that in Japanese and English, is restricted only to the case in which the Theme is considered to lose its identity and change into a completely different entity, as in (101a) and (101b). It follows that Korean exploits the semantic pattern exemplified in (100a) only in very restricted cases. Therefore, assigning a semantic structure like (100a) to double-nominative sentences like (81a) and (83a) is not adequate.

Notice now that the verb *toy* can take a syntactic structure comparable to (100b).

(102) photo-eyse   photocu-ka   toy-essta
      grape-Abl   wine-Nom   become-Past
      'Wine is made from grapes.'

Photo 'grape' is interpreted as Source and *photocu* 'wine' as Theme in (102). However, this pattern is semantically even more restricted than the pattern of (101a). It is allowed only in a sentence in which the NP with *eyse* 'from' is interpreted as 'material' from which the nominative NP is made. Therefore, the following sentences are unacceptable.

(103) a. ?tong-eyse   kum-i   toy-essta
         copper-Abl   gold-Nom   become-Past
         'The gold was made from copper.'

b. *mul-eyse   elum-i   toy-essta
   water-Abl   ice-Nom   become-Past
   'The ice was made from water.'

c. *kyeycel-eyse pom-i   toy-essta
   season-Abl   spring-Nom   become-Past
   'Spring was made from the season.'

d. *John-eyse   sensayng-i   toy-essta
   John-Abl   teacher-Nom   become-Past
   'A teacher was made out of John.'

For the same reason that we could not assign the semantic structure of (100a) to the double-nominative construction with *toy*, we cannot assign it the semantic structure of (100b).

A third possibility is to analyze *toy* in double-nominative constructions as a one-place verb, as in (85), and assign Theme to the "equational" proposition holding between two NPs. For example, (99b) is interpreted thus: the condition that 'John is a teacher' came to exist, a change formalized as follows:

(104) GOcond $(x, y,$ EXIST$)$
      x = BEcond (JOHN, TEACHER)

This semantic analysis seems compatible with the syntactic properties of this type of double-nominative construction. As we observed at the end of 2.1, the A-type double-nominative construction and the B-type double-nominative construction show some syntactic differences. Let us recall the syntactic and semantic structures of the A-type.

(105) Mary-ka   nwun-i   kopta
      Mary-Nom   eye-Nom   beautiful
      'Mary-her eyes are beautiful.'

Syntactic structure
   [$_{S1}$ [$_{NP}$ Mary-Nom] [$_{S2}$ [$_{NP}$ nwun-Nom] [$_{Adj}$ kopta]]]

Semantic structure
   BEcond (MARY, y)
   y = BEcond (MARY'S EYES, BEAUTIFUL)

In (105), the embedded sentence S2 semantically attributes a condition to the subject NP of the matrix sentence S1. As already pointed out, the first nominative postposition is omissible, while the second one is not. In other words, the nominative postposition of the subject of a matrix sentence is omissible while that of the subject of an embedded sentence is not. In

Korean, the nominative and the accusative case-markers can be deleted fairly freely. However, it is a general property of the two postpositions that the more deeply a sentence is embedded, the more difficult it is to delete the postpositions, as shown below.

(106) a. John-i   yelsimi   kongpuha-essta
         John-Nom   hard   study-Past
         'John studied hard.'

   b. John   yelsimi   kongpuha-essta

   c. ?nay-ka   [John   yelsimi   kongpuha-essta-ko]
       I-Nom   John   hard   study-Past-Comp
       sayngkakha-nta
       think
       'I think that John studied hard.'

   d. *nay-ka   [[John kaluchi-n]   haksayng-i
       I-Nom   John teach-Rel   student-Nom
       yelsimi   kongpuha-essta-ko]   sayngkakha-nta
       hard   study-Past-Comp   think
       'I think that the student John taught studied hard.'

I do not have any convincing syntactic explanation of the double-nominative constructions of the B-type. I can only suggest a fairly speculative explanation here. The fact that in the B-type constructions, like (81a), the second nominative marker is omissible, while the first one is not, seems to suggest that the second nominative postposition marks the subject of an embedded sentence. It follows that the syntactic structure of (81a) must be as follows.

(107) [$_{S1}$ [$_{NP}$ [$_{S2}$ [$_{NP}$ John-Nom] [$_{NP}$ sensayng]]-Nom] [$_V$ toy]]

The syntactic representation in (107) indicates that the second nominative postposition in (81a) marks the embedded sentence S2 as the subject of S1. Given the analysis proposed above, the syntactic and semantic structures of the double-nominative construction with *toy* as in (81a) are as follows.

(108) John-i   sensayng-i   toy-essta
      John-Nom   teacher-Nom   become-Past

Syntactic structure
   [$_{S1}$ [$_{NP}$ [$_{S2}$ [$_{NP}$ John-Nom] [$_{NP}$ sensayng]]-Nom] [$_V$ toy]]

Semantic structure
   GOcond ($x, y,$ EXIST)
   x = BEcond (JOHN, TEACHER)

In (108) the correspondence between the syntactic representation and the semantic representation is straightforward. The embedded S2 functioning as the syntactic subject of S1 is interpreted as a static proposition X, which functions semantically as Theme of a dynamic proposition.

Another advantage of our analysis is that there is now no need to say that the verb *toy* is a one-place predicate in (85) and a two-place predicate in (83). The syntactic and semantic structures of (85c) follows.

(109) elum-i   toy-essta
      ice-Nom   become-Past
      'Ice was made.'

Syntactic structure
   [s [NP elum-Nom] [v toy]]

Semantic structure
   GOcond (ICE, EXIST)

The verb *toy* is syntactically defined as a one-place verb that has either an NP or an S as its subject. Semantically, *toy* is defined as a one-place predicate that expresses the 'completion' or 'beginning of existence' of the entity denoted by an NP or the static condition denoted by either an NP or an equational sentence.

Our analysis also accounts for why the Japanese verb *dekiru* 'come out into existence' cannot have a double-nominative construction. Japanese *dekiru* and Korea *toy* are alike in that they express the 'completion' or 'beginning of existence' of an entity, as in the Japanese example (110).

(110) koori-ga   deki-ta
      ice-Nom   be-made-Past
      'Ice was made.'

They differ, however, insofar as *toy* can express the 'completion' or 'beginning of existence' of a static condition, while *dekiru* cannot. See (111).

(111) a. *haru-ga   dekiru
         spring-Nom   be-made

     b. *kisetsu-ga   haru-ga   dekiru
         season-Nom   spring-Nom   be-made

Following the analysis proposed above, the B-type double-nominative sentences in (83) are assigned semantic structures like the following.

(112) a. GOcond $(x, y,$ EXIST$)$
         $x =$ BEcond (SEASON, SPRING)

b. GOcond (*x, y,* EXIST)
    x = BEcond (COPPER, GOLD)

c. GOcond (*x, y,* EXIST)
    x = BEcond (WATER, ICE)

An objection can be made to the analysis of (83b). In (83b), *tong* 'copper' is a previous condition of *kum* 'gold'. Therefore, when some entity goes into a state of being gold, it loses its identity as copper. Thus to say that 'a state of affairs in which copper is gold came to exist' is illogical. It seems to me correct that the semantic representation (112b) is somewhat illogical. However, what I have been pursuing in this section is a "bias" shown by a language in its exploitation of semantic patterns. In other words, when a language is biased towards a particular semantic pattern rather than others, it always reveals some illogicality. It follows that the semantic description of a natural language has to cover this kind of illogicality as well as logicality. The three possibilities for expressing change the Ikegami formalized along the lines of (89), (90), and (91) can be reformalized as (113).

(113) a. GO (*x, y, z*)

b. GO (*z,* WITHOUT *x,* WITH *x*),   GO (*y,* WITH *x,* WITHOUT *x*)

c. GO (*x,* NOT EXIST, EXIST)

Japanese, like English, is biased towards (113a), and therefore expresses a change of condition by analogy with a positional change, exploiting pattern (113a). Similarly, Korean has a bias toward equational interpretations for sentences like (83b). The situation denoted by (83b) can be quite logically expressed by a different verb *nah* 'be born' as in (114).

(114) tong-eyse   kum-i   nah-assta
      copper-Abl   gold-Nom   be born-Past
      'Gold was made from copper.'

However, what is important in understanding the Korean language is to notice that the patterns illustrated in (101), (102), and (114) are very restricted, and that the pattern GOcond ((A = B), *y,* EXIST) is predominant. In contrasting the semantic structures of two languages, it is highly relevant to draw attention to such cases of bias, including illogicalities where they exist.

2.3 Conclusion: Double-nominatives in Korean

1. Korean has two types of double-nominative constructions: the A-type and the B-type. They are distinct syntactically and semantically.

A-type

[s1 NP1-Nom   [s2 NP2-Nom Adj/V]]

BE/GOcond (NP1, y) (y = Goal or Locative)

y = BE/GOcond/poss/posit (NP, Adj/V)

B-type

[s1 [NP [s2 NP1-Nom NP2]-Nom]   [v toy]]

GOcond (x, NOT EXIST, EXIST)

x = BEcond/poss (NP1, NP2)

2. Japanese has the A-type double-nominative construction, but not the B-type.

3. Japanese tends to express change in condition by analogy with a change in location, exploiting the semantic pattern GO (x, y, z). In contrast, Korean tends to express a change of condition as the 'completion' or 'beginning of existence' of an entity or a state of affairs, exploiting the semantic pattern GO (x, y, EXIST). This semantic pattern is very restricted in Japanese. This may be why Japanese does not have the B-type double-nominative construction.

In the contrastive study of Japanese and Korean in the past, only the similarity between the two languages has been emphasized, with the differences described as "trivial." Therefore, the significance of pointing out the fundamental differences between them cannot be overemphasized. The two languages differ drastically in the basic ways they express changes in condition.

Chapter 4
The Passive in Japanese

1. Controversy over the Japanese Passive

Many proposals have been made over the past decade to account for the Japanese passive constructions, which are, or at least look, considerably different from the passive constructions in English. This chapter will examine the traditional distinction between the direct passive and the indirect passive, on which many of these proposals are based, and propose an alternative classification of the Japanese passive.

1.1 Some Characteristics of the Japanese Passive

In Japanese passivization, the suffix *(r)are* (which is sometimes referred to as an auxiliary in traditional Japanese grammar) is added to the verb. The following examples illustrate.

(1) a. karera-ga   Yamada-san-no hon-o   aki-ni
       They-Nom   Mr. Yamada-Gen book-Acc   autumn-in
       syuppansu-ru
       publish-Pres
       'They are publishing Mr. Yamada's book in the autumn.'

   b. Yamada-san-no hon-ga   aki-ni
      Mr. Yamada-Gen book-Nom   autumn-in
      syuppans-are-ru
      publish-Pass-Pres
      'Mr. Yamada's book is being published in the autumn.'

(2) a. John-ga   Mary-o   tatai-ta
       John-Nom   Mary-Acc   hit-Past
       'John hit Mary.'

   b. Mary-ga   John-ni   tatak-are-ta
      Mary-Nom   John-Dat   hit-Pass-Past
      'Mary was hit by John.'

(3) a. John-ga   Mary-ni   kozutumi-o   okut-ta
       John-Nom   Mary-Dat   Parcel-Acc   send-Past
       'John sent a parcel to Mary.'

b. Mary-ga   John-ni   kozutumi-o   oku-rare-ta
      Mary-Nom   John-Dat   parcel-Acc   send-Pass-Past
      'Mary was subjected to John sending a parcel to her.'

(4) a. John-ga   Mary-kara   omotya-o   nusun-da
       John-Nom   Mary-Abl   toy-Acc   steal-Past
       'John stole a toy from Mary.'

   b. Mary-ga   John-ni   omotya-o   nusum-are-ta
      Mary-Nom   John-Dat   toy-Acc   steal-Pass-Past
      'Mary was subjected to John stealing a toy from her.'

(5) a. sensei-ga   Mary-no   musuko-o   sikat-ta
       teacher-Nom   Mary-Gen   son-Acc   scold-Past
       'The teacher scolded Mary's son.'

   b. Mary-ga   sensei-ni   musuko-o   sikar-are-ta
      Mary-Nom   teacher-Dat son-Acc   scold-Pass-Past
      'Mary was subjected to the teacher's scolding her son.'

The following properties of the Japanese passive give rise to dispute. First, passive subjects correspond not only to direct objects but also to various oblique objects of the "corresponding" active sentences. The passive subjects in (1) and (2) correspond to the direct objects. The passive subject corresponds to the indirect object in (3), the object of an ablative postposition in (4) and a possessor NP in (5). A further possibility is that the passive subject corresponds to the "than-NP" in a comparative sentence:

(6) a. John-ga   Mary-yori   sakini   sono hon-o
       John-Nom   Mary-than   previously   that book-Acc
       yon-da
       read-Past
       'John read the book before Mary did.'

   b. Mary-ga   John-ni   sakini   sono hon-o
      Mary-Nom   John-Dat   previously   that book-Acc
      yom-are-ta
      read-Pass-Past
      'Mary was subjected to John's having read the book before her.'

Second, passivization of intransitive constructions like (7) is fully developed. In (7), the passive subject cannot be given any place in the active sentence.

(7) a. ame-ga   hut-ta
       rain-Nom   fall-Past
       'It rained.'

   b. John-ga   ame-ni   hur-are-ta
      John-Nom   rain-Dat   fall-Pass-Past
      'John was rained on.'

Third, the Japanese passive is strongly constrained by animacy. The passive with an inanimate subject is very restricted. The following sentences, for example, are unacceptable.

(8) a. *mado-ga   Mary-ni   ake-rare-ta
       window-Nom   Mary-Dat   open-Pass-Past
       'The window was opened by Mary.'

   b. *ooki-na isi-ga   John-ni   ugokas-are-ta
       big stone-Nom   John-Dat   move-Pass-Past
       'A big stone was moved by John.'

   c. *sono ie-ga   ii ne-de   ur-are-ta
       that house-Nom   good price-at   sell-Pass-Past
       'The house was sold for a good price.'

However, there are many passive sentences with inanimate subjects which are completely acceptable.

(9) a. kono ie-ga   kyonen   tate-rare-ta
       this house-Nom   last-year   build-Pass-Past
       'This house was built last year.'

   b. hon-ga   tana-no ue-ni   ok-are-ta
      book-Nom   shelf-Gen on-Dat   put-Pass-Past
      'The books were put on the shelf.'

   c. kono ronbun-ga   yoku   Chomsky-ni
      this thesis-Nom   often   Chomsky-Dat
      inyoos-are-ru
      quote-Pass-Past
      'This thesis is often quoted by Chomsky.'

Fourth, passive sentences with animate subjects very often entail that the subjects are adversely affected. For instance, the passive sentence in (3b) means that the referent of the subject NP was adversely affected, while the active counterpart is a neutral description of the event in question.

1.2 Approaches from Relational Grammar

1.2.1 Perlmutter and Postal's Universal Characterization of the Passive

Within Relational Grammar, a clause consists of a network of grammatical relations. Among these relations are "subject of," "direct object of," and "indirect object of ." NPs that bear these relations to a particular verb are called its "terms," while other NPs directly dominated by the verb are "nonterms." The major classes of transformation defined in RG are advancement and raising. An advancement rule is defined as one that promotes an NP up the Relational Hierarchy (RH).

RH: Subj > DO > IO > Nonterms

Perlmutter and Postal (1977) have proposed the following universals of passivization.

(10) The direct object of an active clause is the (superficial) subject of the "corresponding" passive.

(11) The subject of an active clause is neither the (superficial) subject nor the (superficial) direct object of the "corresponding" passive.

(10) and (11) taken together have the following consequence:

(12) In the absence of another rule permitting some further nominal to be the direct object of the clause, a passive clause is (superficially) an intransitive clause.

Perlmutter and Postal represent passive clauses in blocks of Relational Networks (RNs), which are called "arcs." For example, the passivization in (13) is represented as in (14).

(13) a. Louise reviewed that book.
     b. That book was reviewed by Louise.

(14) a.

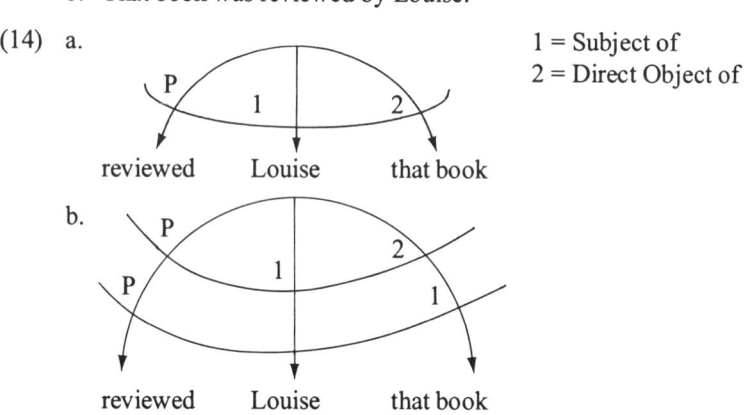

1 = Subject of
2 = Direct Object of

THE PASSIVE IN JAPANESE 87

Our claim is that the RN of every passive clause in any human language has a nominal bearing the 2-relation and 1-relation in successive strata (Perlmutter and Postal 1977:405).

In English, IO is assumed to be promoted to DO before being promoted to become the subject of a passive clause according to the advancement rule.

1.2.2 Shimizu's Proposal

Shimizu (1975), presenting the Japanese evidence against the universal constraints discussed above, shows a "natural way" to modify them to make them consistent with the Japanese data. She claims that the domain of promotion of NPs should be extended to IOs and beneficiaries (Bens) and even to possessors of DOs, pointing out that they correspond to passive subjects in Japanese, as we saw in sentences (3) and (5). She argues that the Japanese passive can directly promote IOs, Bens, and possessors to subject as well as the expected DOs. The following sentences provide an example of the promotion of a possessor NP:

(15) a. doroboo-ga   John-no   zitensya-o   nusun-da
       thief-Nom   John-Gen   bicycle-Acc   steal-Past
       'A thief stole John's bike.'

    b. John-ga   doroboo-ni zitensya-o   nusum-are-ta
       John-Nom   thief-Dat   bicycle-Acc   steal-Pass-Past
       'John had his bike stolen by a thief.'

An analysis of (15b) compatible with Perlmutter and Postal's proposal (which Shimizu argues against; see below) follows.

(i) Raise the possessor to the DO to DO status in conformity with the Relational Succession Law.

       doroboo-ga   John-o   zitensya-?   nusun-da
       thief-Nom   John-Acc   bicycle-?   steal-Past

(ii) Promote the new DO obligatorily to subject via the passive.

       John-ga   doroboo-ni zitensya-? nusum-are-ta
       John-Nom   thief-Dat   bicycle-?   steal-Pass-Past

Shimizu claims that this analysis is inadequate for two reasons. First, step (i) means that the DO *(zitensya)* must, by the Relational Annihilation Law (Perlmutter and Postal 1977:408), cease to be a DO. But after passivization applies in step (ii), *zitensya* remains DO. Second, the intermediate step (i) is ungrammatical. Shimizu proposes an alternative analysis on the basis of the topic–comment construction. In her view, the derivation of (15b) is as follows:

(15) a. doroboo-ga   John-no   zitensya-o   nusun-da
         thief-Nom   John-Gen   bicycle-Acc   steal-Past

The possessor NP is topicalized, yielding (15a').

(15) a.' John-wa   doroboo-ga   zitensya-o   nusun-da
         John-Top   thief-Nom   bicycle-Acc   steal-Past
         'As for John, a thief stole his bike.'

Then (15a') is passivized, demoting the original subject to "passive agent" as in (15b').

(15) b.' John-wa   doroboo-ni   zitensya-o   nusum-are-ta
         John-Top   thief-Dar   bicycle   steal-Pass-Past

Shimizu's proposal is not justifiable either as part of a universal theory of the passive or as part of a theory of the Japanese passive. First, the topicalized sentence in (15a') is hardly acceptable. Second, in Japanese, NPs other than DO, IO, Ben, and possessor can be passive subjects, as pointed out in 1.1. Of what use to universal grammar or to Japanese grammar would be a rule so weakened as to say that virtually any oblique NP in an active sentence can be the subject of a corresponding passive sentence? The third deficiency of Shimizu's analysis is that it meets serious difficulty when it is applied to sentences like (7b), whose subject has no corresponding NP in the active. Should sentences of this type be excluded from the category of passive? I cannot find any syntactic or semantic reason to do so.

1.2.3 Demotional Passive

Shimizu's analysis is supported by Keenan (1975). Both Keenan (1975) and Comrie (1977) take examples from several languages in which the passive involves subject deletion or subject demotion, but lacks object promotion, They use these as evidence that the demotion of subject precedes the promotion of direct object. (The following examples are from Comrie 1977.)

Latin

(a) Milites   acriter   pugnaverunt
    soldiers   fiercely   fought
    'The soldiers fought fiercely.'

(b) Acriter   (a militibus)   pugnatum est
    fiercely   by soldiers   fought is
    'There was fierce fighting (by the soldiers).'

Welsh

(a) Aeth   llawer   yno   ynyr haf
    went   many   there   in the summer
    'Many people went there in summer.'

(b) Eir   yno   (gen lawer)   ynyr haf
    was-gone   there   by many   in the summer
    [Comrie provides no translation.]

Japanese sentences like (16), according to Keenan, are problematic for any promotional analysis of the passive "since there is no underlying source in which the derived subject ... has a grammatical relation to the verb." (Keenan 1975:348).

(16) Taroo-ga   Hanako-ni   nige-rare-ta
     Taroo-Nom   Hanako-Dat   run-away-Pass-Past
     'Taroo was run away on by Hanako.'

A topicalized sentence along the lines proposed by Shimizu is advocated as "the most plausible underlying source" (Keenan 1975:348).

(17) *Taroo-wa   Hanako-ga   nige-ta
     Taroo-Top   Hanako-Nom   run-away-Past
     'As for Taroo, Hanako ran away from him.'

Passivization of (17) entails the demotion of the subject *Hanako* to yield (16). However, as already pointed out, (17) is unacceptable as a Japanese sentence. If this kind of topicalization should be permitted, topicalization would be little short of almighty and could be the underlying source of any construction. An NP can normally be topicalized in case it has any semantic correlation with the predicate or the proposition as a whole.

(18) a. John-wa   ringo-o   tabe-ta
       John-Top   apple-Acc   eat-Past
       'As for John, he ate an apple.'

    b. sono ringo-wa   John-ga   tabe-ta
       that apple-Top   John-Nom   eat-Past
       'As for the apple, John ate it.'

    c. kyoo-wa   John-ga   gakkoo-ni   it-ta
       today-Top   John-Nom   school-Dat   go-Past
       'As for today, John went to school.'

What makes topicalization possible in (18a) and (18b) is the underlying semantic relation 'John ate an/the apple'. *Kyoo* 'today' in (18c) can be topicalized since it has a semantic correlation with the proposition 'John went to school'. In (19a), however, the topicalized NP *John* cannot be supposed to have any semantic relation with the predicate *huru* 'to rain' or the proposition *ame-ga huru* 'it rains' before passivization applies.

(19) a. *John-wa   ame-ga   hut-ta
         John-Top   rain-Nom   fall-Past
         'As for John, it rained.'

     b. John-wa   ame-ni   hur-are-ta
         John-Top   rain-Dat   fall-Pass-Past
         'As for John, he was rained on.'

Shimizu holds that universal grammar should be modified to be consistent with the Japanese passive. Keenan, in turn, forces Japanese to have unacceptable underlying sources to be consistent with the universality of the demotional passive.

From the argument so far, it should be clear that the Japanese passive cannot be adequately captured by an approach that asks what kinds of NPs in an active sentence can be the subject of the corresponding passive sentence.

1.3 Approaches from Transformational Grammar: Direct Passive and Indirect Passive

The Japanese passive has been studied in terms of a traditional and widespread distinction between the direct passive and the indirect passive. A direct passive sentence is a sentence whose subject corresponds to the direct object of the corresponding active sentence, as in (1) and (2). In (2b), for instance, *Mary* is directly affected by the action taken by *John*. An indirect passive sentence is syntactically defined as a passive sentence whose subject corresponds to NPs that are not the direct object of the active sentence—as in (4), (5), and (6)—or does not have any corresponding NP in the active sentence—as in (7). The indirect passives in (4b), (5b), (6b) are formally distinct from direct passives in that the former contain accusative NPs. It is assumed that the indirect passive differs semantically from the direct passive in that the former means that the passive subject is indirectly affected by an action or an event. The indirect passive sentence (5b), for example, means that the subject (*Mary*) is affected as a consequence of the event of the teacher scolding her son.

Among many transformation analyses, the analysis proposed by Kuno (1973), which was adopted by Teramura (1982), seems to have gained widespread acceptance. According to their analyses, the direct passive and the indirect passive have different underlying sources. An indirect passive like (5b), cited again below, is derived from an underlying structure involving two sentences.

(5) b. Mary-ga   sensei-ni   musuko-o   sikar-are-ta
       Mary-Nom   teacher-Dat   son-Acc   scold-Pass-Past
       'Mary was subjected to the teacher's scolding her son.'

(20)
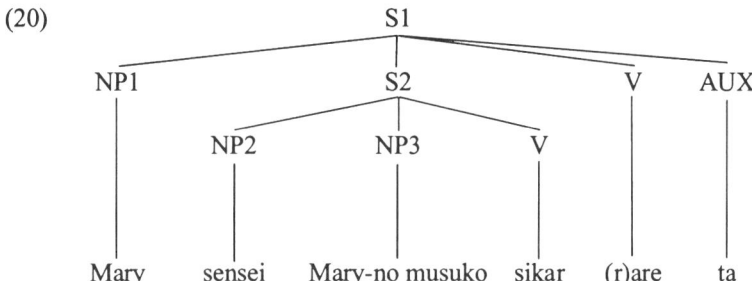

A direct passive sentence like (2b) is derived by applying a permutation transformation to a simplified underlying structure as in (21).

(21)
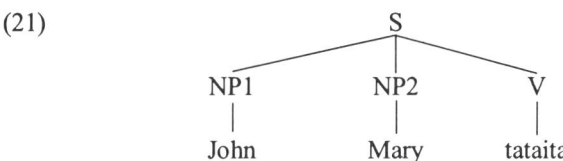

Before examining the analyses based on the distinction between the direct passive and the indirect passive in detail, I will compare the analysis of the indirect passive shown in (20) with the analysis proposed by Shimizu and Keenan. The former has an advantage over the latter since it presents no problem of determining where the passive subject comes from. NP1 in (20) does not belong to the active sentential counterpart.

One reason given by Kuno (1973), Teramura (1982), and many others for admitting the distinction between the direct passive and the indirect passive is that the indirect passives are semantically adverse passives, while the direct passives are the pure or neutral passives, like the passive in English. However, the correspondence between the formal distinction and the semantic distinction is called into serious question if we examine the following sentences.

(22) a. kyuuzyotai-ga   John-o   hakkensi-ta
        rescue-party-Nom   John-Acc   find-Past
        'The rescue party found John.'

b. John-ga   kyuuzyotai-ni   hakkens-are-ta
   John-Nom   rescue-party-Dat   find-Pass-Past
   'John was found by the rescue party.'

(23) a. John-ga   Mary-o   tukamae-ta
        John-Nom   Mary-Acc   catch-Past
        'John caught Mary.'

   b. Mary-ga   John-ni   tukamae-rare-ta
      Mary-Nom   John-Dat   catch-Pass-Past
      'Mary was subjected to John's catching her.'

(24) a. John-ga   Mary-o   mi-ta
        John-Nom   Mary-Acc   see-Past
        'John saw Mary.'

   b. Mary-ga   John-ni   mi-rare-ta
      Mary-Nom   John-Dat   see-Pass-Past
      'Mary was subjected to John's seeing her.'

Sentence (22b) can be regarded as a neutral passive sentence. However, the direct passive sentences (23b) and (24b) are most likely to be interpreted as expressing adverse affectedness of the subjects. This suggests that these direct passive sentences are semantically homogeneous with the following indirect passive sentences, which also imply that the subjects are adversely affected.

(25) Mary-ga   John-ni   ude-o   tukam-are-ta
     Mary-Nom   John-Dat   arm-Acc   catch-Pass-Past
     'Mary was subjected to John's catching her arm.'

(26) Mary-ga   John-ni   heya-o   mi-rare-ta
     Mary-Nom   John-Dat   room-Acc   see-Pass-Past
     'Mary was subjected to John's seeing her room.'

The analyses proposed by Kuno and Teramura also cannot explain why direct passive sentences like (27b) are unacceptable.

(27) a. John-ga   tukue-o   tatai-ta
        John-Nom   desk-Acc   hit-Past
        'John hit the desk.'

   b. *tukue-ga   John-ni/ni-yotte   tatak-are-ta
       desk-Nom   John-Dat/relying on   hit-Pass-Past
       'The desk was hit by John.'

The unacceptability of (27b) comes from the semantic contradiction that an inanimate subject *tukue* 'desk' is treated as if it were adversely affected. If we assume that the direct passive sentences (23b), (24b), and (27b) are semantically homogeneous with the indirect passive, then the unacceptability of (27b) can be accounted for because the indirect passive, unlike the direct passive, does not allow an inanimate subject, and very often entails that the subject is adversely affected, as already pointed out.

(28) *tukue-ga   John-ni/ni-yotte   asi-o   tatak-are-ta
     desk-Nom   John-Dat/relying on   leg-Acc   hit-Pass-Past
     'The desk was subjected to John's hitting its leg.'

The passive sentence (28), like (27b), is acceptable only when the subject is interpreted as being personified.

The analyses of the Japanese passive in terms of the distinction between direct and indirect passives offer no explanation for why some direct passives, like (23b) and (24b), require an adversative interpretation, while others, like (1b) and (9a, b, c) admit a nonadverse interpretation. In (9c), for instance, there is no reading in which the subject NP is badly affected by Chomsky. The implication of (9c) is that the thesis is well known, excellent, or perhaps even foolish. Masuoka (1982) calls this type of construction the "attributive passive" and Klaiman (1982b) calls it "nonaffective." Klaiman correctly points out that sentences like (9c) are acceptable because the action is viewed differently—not as a specific deed or event, but as a process whose effects are attributed to the subject. Study of the data cited above suggests that the traditional notion of the direct passive encompasses constructions which are semantically heterogeneous: some are semantically homogeneous with the indirect passive, and some are distinct from it.

In the next section, we will propose a more comprehensive description of the passive in Japanese.

2. Semantic Approaches to the Japanese Passive

2.1 Traditional Approaches

In Japanese, passive constructions are formally marked by *(r)are*. This marker is referred to variously as a "formative," a "higher verb," and so forth. However, it is often called the "passive auxiliary" in the traditional grammar of Japanese. The traditional Japanese grammarians were not so "westernized" as more recent grammarians, and in their analysis of "auxiliaries of voice," did not confine themselves to the opposition between the active and the passive. There are two formally distinct voice auxiliaries: *(r)are* and *(s)ase*. The former indicates passive, potentiality, and spontaneity, while the latter indicates causativity. The passive auxiliary *(r)are* and the causative *(s)ase* have been considered to stand in opposition to each other, while nevertheless sharing common traits.

Let us compare the following passive and causative sentences.

(29) a. Mary-ga   John-ni   omotya-o   nusum-are-ta
Mary-Nom   John-Dat   toy-Acc   steal-Pass-Past
'Mary was subjected to John's stealing a toy from her.'

b. Mary-ga   John-ni   omotya-o   nusum-ase-ta
Mary-Nom   John-Dat   toy-Acc   steal-Cause-Past
'Mary made/let John steal a toy.'

(30) a. Mary-ga   sensei-ni   musuko-o   sikar-are-ta
Mary-Nom   teacher-Dat   son-Acc   scold-Pass-Past
'Mary was subjected to the teacher's scolding her son.'

b. Mary-ga   sensei-ni   musuko-o   sikar-ase-ta
Mary-Nom   teacher-Dat   son-Acc   scold-Cause-Past
'Mary made/let the teacher scold Mary's (or the teacher's) son.'

(31) a. John-ga   Mary-ni   kaer-are-ta
John-Nom   Mary-Dat   go-home-Pass-Past
'John was subjected to Mary's going home.'

b. John-ga   Mary-o/ni   kaer-ase-ta
John-Nom   Mary-Acc/Dat   go-home-Cause-Past
'John made/let Mary go home.'

(32) a. John-ga   ame-ni   hur-are-ta
John-Nom   rain-Dat   fall-Pass-Past
'John was rained on.'

b. John-ga   ame-o   hur-ase-ta
John-Nom   rain-Acc   fall-Cause-Past
'John made it rain.'

(33) a. watasi-ga   musuko-ni   sin-are-ta
I-Nom   son-Dat   die-Pass-Past
'I was subjected to my son's death.'

b. watasi-ga   musuko-o   sin-ase-ta
I-Nom   son-Acc   die-Cause-Past
'I made/let my son die.'

The causative sentences are obtained merely by substituting *(s)ase* for *(r)are* in (29), (30), and (31), and by the additional replacement of the case marker *ni* with *o* in (32) and (33). In (31b), the causee can have *o* or *ni*. If the accusative *o* is chosen, the sentence is most likely to be given the interpretation with 'make', while if the dative *ni* is chosen, it is given the interpretation with 'let'.

The Japanese causative can be used to express the meaning of agentive causation or permissive causation, which can be represented by CAUSE and LET respectively. Sentence (33b) is therefore ambiguous between the two interpretations: 'I made my son die', and 'I did not prevent my son from dying'. The causative meaning of (33b) is often so neutralized that it can be felt to be almost equivalent semantically to the passive sentence (33a). In this case, the son's death (from illness, in war, etc.) is described both in (33a) and (33b) as being beyond the control of the speaker. However, if the speaker felt any responsibility for this son's death, he would say (33b). If he says (33a), he emphasizes his being affected by his son's death. Yoshida (1971:99) points out that one and the same action or event can be described either in the passive or in the causative. He writes (1971:80), "The causative and the passive, mediated by the sense of 'permission' and 'not preventing', are in such a relation as that between the two sides of a paper."

It has been pointed out in the previous sections that attempts to correlate the active and the passive in the same way as in English encounter serious difficulty because many Japanese passive sentences do not have any semantically equivalent active counterparts. In English, the active and the passive voice "make it possible to view the action of a sentence in two ways, without change in the fact reported" (Quirk et al. 1972:801). In other words, the active and the passive are equivalent in their factual meaning in spite of the formal transformation triggered in a focus-shifting process. In many cases, this kind of semantic equivalence between the active and the passive does not exist in Japanese. If equivalence of factual meaning exists in a voice opposition, it should be sought between the causative and the passive, as in (33).

2.2 Causative Constructions and the Passive of Interest

Let us consider the relation between the following causative and indirect passive sentences.

(34) a. Mary-ga   kaet-ta
     Mary-Nom   go-home-Past
     'Mary went home.'

b. John-ga   Mary-o/ni   kaer-ase-ta
   John-Nom   Mary-Acc/Dat   go-home-Cause-Past
   'John made/let Mary go home.'

c. John-ga   Mary-ni   kaer-are-ta
      John-Nom   Mary-Dat   go-home-Pass-Past
      'John was subjected to Mary's going home.'

The (b) sentence can be derived from the (a) sentence by the introduction of a new causative agent (*John*). Similarly, the (c) sentence can be derived from the (a) sentence by the introduction of a new participant (*John*) who is affected by the event of 'Mary's going home'. Sentences (34b) and (34c) are similar in that they share a proposition denoted by (34a) and have additional participants that are involved somehow in the direct action described in (34a). The sentences differ in that the involvement is active in (34b) but passive in (34c). Ikegami (1981a) points out that the relation between the causative and the passive in Japanese can be described in terms of "control" and "independence." In his analysis, the relation between the causative and the passive in (34) is stated in terms of the relation between 'John's control over Mary' (C) and 'Mary's independence' (I).

(35) a. John-ga   Mary-o   kaer-ase-ta
         'John made Mary go home.'
         C > I

      b. John-ga   Mary-ni   kaer-ase-ta
         'John let Mary go home.'
         C > I

      c. John-ga   Mary-ni   kaer-are-ta
         'John was subjected to Mary's going home.'
         C < I

The semantic structures of (35a–c), following Ikegami, are respectively represented in (36a–c).

(36) a. CAUSE (JOHN, (S))
      b. LET (JOHN, (S))
      c. GET (JOHN, (S))

The S stands for the embedded proposition 'Mary went home', which is represented as GO (MARY, y, HOME). The same explanation applies to the causative and the indirect passive sentences in (30). When the verb is transitive, as in (30b), the causee can only have the dative postposition. This causes an ambiguity between the CAUSE interpretation and the LET interpretation. Sentence (30b) is also ambiguous as to whether *musuko* 'son' belongs to *Mary* or *sensei* 'teacher'. The passive sentence (30a) means that Mary was affected by the action of the teacher scolding some individual. Therefore the most natural interpretation is that Mary was affected by the action because the individual being scolded was a person related to her or sharing a common interest with her. This is why *zibun* in (37) sounds redundant.

(37) Mary-ga   sensei-ni   zibun-no   musuko-o   sikar-are-ta
Mary-Nom teacher-Dat self-Gen   son-Acc   scold-Pass-Past
'Mary was subjected to the teacher's scolding her son.'

The foregoing shows that the passive sentence (30a) is in opposition to the causative sentence (30b) on the reading that Mary's son was scolded. Thus the causative and passive sentences in (30) can be derived from (38) by the introduction of a causative or permissive agent and an affected participant, respectively.

(38) sensei-ga   Mary-no   musuko-o   sikat-ta
teacher-Nom Mary-Gen   son-Acc   scold-Past
'The teacher scolded Mary's son.'

We have so far stated somewhat vaguely that the introduced participant in an indirect passive is "affected" or "affected as a consequence of an event." However, the way in which the subject of the indirect passive is affected differs somewhat from the way in which the participants emphasized in the following sentences are affected.

(39) a. John hit *Mary*.
b. John hit *the door*.
c. John gave a book *to Mary*.

These participants are affected by actions that are directed at them. This type of affectedness, involving the participant toward which an action is directed, will be called "objective affectedness." In contrast, the affectedness expressed in indirect passive sentences like the (a) sentences in (29)–(33) is independent of the directedness of the action or event. These passive sentences mean that the subject NPs are emotionally affected as a consequence of events that are not necessarily directed at them. In the situation denoted by (29a), John may or may not have stolen Mary's toy with the intention of affecting her. However, what (29c) expresses is that Mary was adversely affected as a consequence of it. In (30a), Mary is supposed to be adversely affected because the person scolded by the teacher happened to be her son. In (32a), there is no necessary relation between raining and John's being affected. Rather, (32a) implies that John was affected by the rain because of his own conditions, his plan for a picnic, his having no umbrella, his hating rain, and so on. These passive sentences are used when the speaker describes an event from the viewpoint of a particular individual denoted by the subject NP. Therefore, the affectedness expressed in these passive sentences may be called "empathy-based affectedness." If we describe the relation between an event and objective affectedness in logical terms as a cause–effect relation, then we can describe the relation between an event and empathy-based affectedness as a reason–effect relation. The cause is a necessary and sufficient condition for producing the effect, while the reason may just be a necessary condition that hastens the effect. Our analysis is compatible with the fact that the subject of an indirect passive sentence must be animate, and typically human. As already pointed out, this type of passive is used when the speaker describes an event in terms of the concerns of a participant denoted by the subject NP. This participant must therefore be animate, and typically human. It follows that this participant is described by the speaker as an individual who perceives the effect. We therefore assign the semantic role Experiencer to this participant. We can now define the derivations of the causative and the indirect passive sentences in terms of the introduction of causative or permissive Agent and Experiencer, respectively.

(40) Active
→ Causative: causative or permissive Agent introduced as the subject
→ Indirect passive: Experiencer introduced as the subject

However, the analysis that Japanese passive sentences are derived from active sentences by the introduction of an Experiencer seems to fail to account for so-called direct passive sentences like (41b).

(41) a. John-ga Mary-o tatai-ta
John-Nom Mary-Acc hit-Past
'John hit Mary.'

b. Mary-ga John-ni tatak-are-ta
Mary-Nom John-Dat hit-Pass-Past
'Mary was subjected to John's hitting her.'

Japanese transformational grammarians insist that (41b) is a "pure" or "neutral" passive expressing the fact that the subject is directly affected by the action, not as an indirect consequence of it, and that (41b) is derived from the corresponding active sentence by NP permutation. However, if passive sentences like (41b) are supposed to be derived by NP permutation, the unacceptability of sentence (27), repeated here as (42), cannot be properly accounted for.

(42) a. John-ga   tukue-o   tatai-ta
　　　 John-Nom   desk-Acc   hit-Past
　　　 'John hit the desk.'

　　 b. *tukue-ga   John-ni-(yotte)   tatak-are-ta
　　　　 desk-Nom   John-Dat   hit-Pass-Past
　　　 'The desk was hit by John.'

Under the permutation analysis, the frequency of transitive sentences with inanimate direct objects ought to yield a huge number of passive sentences with inanimate subjects like (43). However, this is not the case.

(43) *ringo-ga   John-ni-(yotte)   tabe-rare-ta
　　　 apple-Nom   John-Dat   eat-Pass-Past
　　　 'The apple was eaten by John.'

The reason why passive sentences like (42b) and (43) sound odd must be the fact that the inanimate subjects are described as if they were emotionally affected by the actions. The active sentence (41a) indicates that the direct object *Mary* was objectively affected, but it does not necessarily say that she was emotionally affected as a consequence of being objectively affected. Our assumption, rather, is that in the passive sentence (41b), Mary is described as being affected emotionally in consequence of the event that John hit her. Our analysis thus explains why (42b) sounds odd, and also explains data like the following.

(44) a. John-ga   Mary-o   mi-ta
　　　 John-Nom   Mary-Acc   see-Past
　　　 'John saw Mary.'

　　 b. Mary-ga   John-ni   mi-rare-ta
　　　 Mary-Nom   John-Dat   see-Pass-Past
　　　 'Mary was subjected to John's seeing her.'

(45) a. John-ga   Mary-ni   kozutumi-o   okut-ta
　　　 John-Nom   Mary-Dat   parcel-Acc   send-Past
　　　 'John sent a parcel to Mary.'

　　 b. Mary-ga   John-ni   kozutumi-o   okur-are-ta
　　　 Mary-Nom   John-Dat   parcel-Acc   send-Pass-Past
　　　 'Mary was subjected to John's sending a parcel to her.'

The active sentence (44a) does not say that Mary was objectively affected, while the passive sentence (44b) entails that Mary was adversely affected as a consequence of John's seeing her. It follows that this type of passive is possible without the reading that the passive subject is objectively affected. Sentence (45a) entails that Mary was objectively affected since the action of John's sending a parcel is directed at her and the sentence does not mean that she was adversely affected. In spite of this, the passive sentence (45b) entails that she was adversely affected as a consequence of the event. Furthermore, (45b) is formally identical with the typical indirect passive. The foregoing suggests that this type of passive is independent of objective affectedness and encompasses both the traditional indirect passive as well as some direct passive constructions.

We have so far argued that the distinction between direct and indirect passive has no semantic basis. Nor is the distinction between them always clear syntactically.

(46) a. John-ga   Mary-ni   hinans-are-ta
       John-Nom   Mary-Dat   blame-Pass-Past
       'John was subjected to Mary's blaming him.'

   b. John-ga   Mary-ni   kao-o   tatak-are-ta
      John-Nom   Mary-Dat   face-Acc   hit-Pass-Past
      'John was subjected to Mary's hitting his face.'

   c. John-ga   Mary-ni   musuko-o   tatak-are-ta
      John-Nom   Mary-Dat   son-Acc   hit-Pass-Past
      'John was subjected to Mary's hitting his son.'

   d. John-ga   ame-ni   hur-are-ta
      John-Nom   rain-Dat   fall-Pass-Past
      'John was rained on.'

Sentence (46a) is defined as a typical direct or neutral passive sentence, while (46c) and (46d) are indirect passive sentences. Sentence (46b), however, is problematic. In the situation denoted by this sentence, John was directly affected by the action taken by Mary, even though the sentence is identical to typical indirect passives. Moreover, if (46a) is permutationally obtained from the active counterpart *Mary-ga John-o hinansita* 'Mary blamed John', then the same transformation should be applicable to (47a) below.

(47) a. Mary-ga   John-no   kao-o   tatai-ta
       Mary-Nom   John-Gen   face-Acc   hit-Past
       'Mary hit John's face.'

   b. ?John-no   kao-ga   Mary-ni   tatak-are-ta
      John-Gen   face-Nom   Mary-Dat   hit-Pass-Past
      'John's face was hit by Mary.'

The only possible passive sentence is (46b).

The data examined above show that some direct passives are syntactically or semantically homogeneous with the so-called indirect passive. It follows that these passive constructions are derived by the introduction of Experiencer as a new subject. Semantically this type of passive depends on empathy-based affectedness rather than objective affectedness, that is, these sentences are used when the speaker describes an event in terms of the interest of the participant denoted by the subject. For this reason, we may call this type of passive the "passive of interest." The definition of the passive of interest recalls Lakoff's remark on the *get*-passive in English.

> The *get* passive in English, unlike the *be* passive, is frequently used to reflect the attitude of the speaker toward the events described in the sentence: whether he feels they are good or bad, or reflect well or poorly on him or the superficial subject of the sentence (for whom he thus expresses implicit sympathy) (Lakoff 1971:154).

Lakoff holds that if the speaker is a department chairman, he can use *get* in (48a); if, however, he is a newscaster, he will in all probability be restricted to *be*, as in (48b).

(48) a. This department is going to hell! Six linguists got arrested for possession of marijuana.

   b. At the University of Throgg this afternoon, six linguists were arrested for possession of marijuana.

The formal difference between the indirect passive and the direct passive sentences studied in this section, which are now subsumed under the label "passive of interest," can be accounted for by a single deletion rule.

(49) John-ga   [Mary-ga   John-o   hinans-]   are-ta
     John-Nom   Mary-Nom   John-Acc   blame   Pass-Past

→ John-ga   Mary-ni   *(deleted)*   hinans-are-ta

(50) John-ga   [Mary-ga   John-no   musuko-o   tatak-]   are-ta
     John-Nom   Mary-Nom   John-Gen   son-Acc   hit   Pass-Past

→ John-ga   Mary-ni   *(deleted)*   musuko-o   tatak-are-ta

The semantic contents of (46a–d) seem to form a continuum with three strata. The first stratum includes (a); the second, (b) and (c); and the third, (d). The basic structure of the passive of interest is thus:

NP1-ga   NP2-ni   (NP3-o)   V-(r)are
Nom   Dat   Acc   Pass

NP3 is not realized when it is completely identical with NP1, but the slot for NP3 is filled by a lexical item when NP1 is partially identical with NP3. The former case may be referred to as complete reflexivization and the latter as possessive reflexivization. In (46a), NP1 and NP3 are in a completely reflexive relation and therefore NP3 is not realized. This subtype of the passive of interest may be called the "complete reflexive type." In the second stratum, to which (46b) and (46c) belong, NP1 and NP3 are in the possessive reflexive relation, and therefore NP3 is realized. We refer to this subtype as the "possessive reflexive type." In (46d), belonging to the third stratum, there is no reflexive relation between the subject NP and the NP in the embedded sentence, as shown in (51).

(51) a. John-ga   [ame-ga   hur-]   are-ta
       John-Nom   rain-Nom   fall   Pass-Past

    b. John-ga   ame-ni   hur-are-ta
       John-Nom   rain-Dat   fall-Pass-Past
       'John was rained on.'

Thus, the passive of interest has three subtypes, as follows:

(52) *Passive of interest*
    a. Complete reflexive type
    b. Possessive reflexive type
    c. Nonreflexive type

One question has been deliberately avoided, namely, why the passive of interest is biased towards adverse affectedness. Japanese, like many other languages, has markers for beneficial affectedness in a simple active clause, while lacking such markers for adverse affectedness. Neutral expressions such as (53a) can be converted into expressions of beneficial affectedness by forming a gerundive verb, V + *te-ageru* (V + 'give'), as in (53b).

(53) a. John-ga   Mary-ni   kozutumi-o   okut-ta
       John-Nom   Mary-Dat   parcel-Acc   send-Past
       'John sent a parcel to Mary.'

    b. John-ga   Mary-ni   kozutumi-o   okut-te-age-ta
       John-Nom   Mary-Dat   parcel-Acc   send-ing-give-Past
       'John sent a parcel to Mary (for her benefit).'

However, there is no way to express adverse affectedness explicitly in a simple active clause. There is also a passivelike marker *te-morau* 'receive', which is attached to verbs to express beneficial affectedness.

(54) a. Mary-ga   John-ni   tatai-te-morat-ta
       Mary-Nom   John-Dat   hit-ing-receive-Past
       'Mary had John hit her (for her benefit).'

   b. Mary-ga   John-ni   kozutumi-o   okut-te-morat-ta
      Mary-Nom   John-Dat   parcel-Acc   send-ing-receive-Past
      'Mary had John send a parcel for (instead of) her.'

I speculate that the availability of means to explicitly express beneficial affectedness makes the *(r)are* form, although formally a simple passive marker, biased toward adverse affectedness.

2.3 Anticausative Passive

Our analysis, according to which the passive in Japanese is derived by the introduction of an Experiencer who is described by the speaker as being affected as a consequence of an event, fails to account for the following passive sentences with inanimate subjects.

(55) a. mura-no hitobito-ga   kono tera-o
       village-Gen people-Nom   this temple-Acc
       hyakunen-mae-ni   kensetusi-ta
       100-years-ago   build-Past
       'People of the village built this temple 100 years ago.'

   b. kono tera-ga   hyakunen-mae-ni
      this temple-Nom   100-years-ago
      (mura-no hitobito-ni-yotte)   kensetus-are-ta
      village-Gen people-relying-on   build-Pass-Past
      'This temple was built (by people of the village) 100 years ago.'

(56) a. John-ga   mondai-no naihu-o
       John-Nom   in-question knife-Acc
       kono ki-no sita-ni   sute-ta
       this tree-Gen under-Loc   dump-Past
       'John dumped the knife in question under this tree.'

   b. mondai-no naihu-ga   (John-ni-yotte)
      in question knife-Nom   John-relying-on
      kono ki-no sita-ni   sute-rare-ta
      this tree-Gen under-Loc   dump-Pass-Past
      'The knife in question was dumped (by John) under this tree.'

(57) a. Mary-ga   syokuzensyu-tosite   syerii-o
       Mary-Nom   aperitif-as   sherry-Acc
       eran-da
       choose-Past
       'Mary chose sherry as an aperitif.'

   b. syerii-ga   (Mary-ni-yotte)   syokuzensyu-tosite
       sherry-Nom   Mary-relying-on   aperitif-as
       erab-are-ta
       choose-Pass-Past
       'Sherry was chosen as an aperitif (by Mary).'

(58) a. John-ga   tana-kara   hon-o   orosi-ta
       John-Nom   shelf-Abl   book-Acc   lower-Past
       'John lowered books from the shelf.'

   b. hon-ga   (John-ni-yotte) tana-kara   oros-are-ta
       book-Nom   John-relying-on shelf-Abl   lower-Pass-Past
       'Books were lowered from the shelf (by John).'

This type of passive is distinct from the passive of interest in two characteristics. First, this type is restricted mainly to factitive verbs, while the passive of interest applies to any type of verb. The thematic relations of the sentences in (55a, b) through (58a, b) are represented in (59a, b) through (62a, b), respectively.

(59) a. CAUSE (PEOPLE OF THE VILLAGE, GOcond (THIS TEMPLE, y, EXIST))
   b. GOcond (THIS TEMPLE, y, EXIST)

(60) a. CAUSE (JOHN, GOposit (THE KNIFE IN QUESTION, y, UNDER THE TREE))
   b. GOposit (THE KNIFE IN QUESTION, y, UNDER THE TREE)

(61) a. CAUSE (MARY, GOposs (SHERRY, ALL POSSIBLE APERITIFS, MARY))
   b. GOposs (SHERRY, ALL POSSIBLE APERITIFS, MARY)

(62) a. CAUSE (JOHN, GOposit (BOOKS, SHELF, DOWN))
   b. GOposit (BOOKS, SHELF, DOWN)

Second, this type of passive cannot have the agentive phrase marked by the dative *ni*. The agentlike NP of a passive sentence of this type is sometimes marked by *ni-yotte* 'relying on', 'due to'. It is often claimed in studies of the Japanese passive within transformational grammar (cf. Inoue 1976, Kuroda 1980) that the passive agent is marked by *ni* when the subject is animate and by *ni-yotte* when the subject is inanimate. Marking a passive agent with *ni-yotte* is a fairly recent development and it is still not used very often in ordinary conversation. It is mainly used in sophisticated writing, such as newspaper articles, academic theses, and so forth. The passive sentences (56b), (57b), and (58b) sound artificial with NP + *ni-yotte*, as if they are literal translations of sentences in European languages. These facts suggest that the primary function of this type of passive is to eliminate the causative Agent, or background it, and describe a change undergone by the Theme. This type of passive can therefore be characterized semantically as an anticausative or inchoative sentence. We may therefore call these passive sentences "anticausative passives."

There is another type of anticausative construction that is similar to the anticausative passive. Many of the factitive verbs of Japanese show a fairly systematic opposition with intransitive counterparts.

Intransitive	*Transitive*
agar- 'rise'	age- 'raise'
simar- 'get shut'	sime- 'shut'
kudak-e- 'get crushed'	kudak- 'crush'
kir-e- 'get cut'	kir- 'cut'

These intransitive verbs have been referred to in traditional Japanese grammars as "spontaneous verbs" because they strongly entail that a spontaneous change takes place. The oppositions between the transitive and the intransitive exemplified above are semantically analyzed as follows.

Intransitive	*Transitive*
GO (x, y, z)	CAUSE $(w,$ GO $(x, y, z))$

Our formalization cannot differentiate this type of intransitive construction from the anticausative passive. Let us consider the following examples.

(63) *Active transitive*
    a. booto-ga   densen-o   kit-ta
       rioter-Nom electric-wire-Acc cut-Past
       'Rioters cut the electric wire.'

    a.' CAUSE (RIOTERS, GOcond (THE ELECTRIC WIRE, y, CUT))

Anticausative passive
    b. densen-ga   kir-are-ta
       electric-wire-Nom   cut-Pass-Past
       'The electric wire was cut.'

    b.' GOcond (THE ELECTRIC WIRE, y, CUT)

Spontaneous
    c. densen-ga   kir-e-ta
       electric-wire-Nom   get-cut-Past
       'The electric wire got cut.'

c.′ GOcond (THE ELECTRIC WIRE, *y*, CUT)

(64) *Active transitive*
    a. booto-ga   mado-garasu-o   wat-ta
       rioter-Nom   window-glass-Acc break-Past
       'Rioters broke the window glass.'

    a.′ CAUSE (RIOTERS, GOcond (THE WINDOW GLASS, *y*, BROKEN))

    Anticausative passive
    b. mado-garasu-ga   war-are-ta
       window-glass-Nom break-Pass-Past
       'The window glass was broken.'

    b.′ GOcond (THE WINDOW GLASS, *y*, BROKEN)

    Spontaneous
    c. mado-garasu-ga   war-e-ta
       window-glass-Nom get-broken-Past
       'The window glass broke.'

    c.′ GOcond (THE WINDOW GLASS, *y*, BROKEN)

The difference between anticausative passives like (63b) and (64b) and spontaneous sentences like (63c) and (64c) lies in the fact that the former imply the existence of an Agent, while the latter denotes that change takes place spontaneously. This difference between the anticausative passive and the spontaneous sentences can be described in Halliday's terms as one between "agent-oriented" and "process-oriented" clauses. This analysis is supported by the fact that an anticausative passive sentence can have an Agent phrase marked by *ni-yotte*, while a spontaneous sentence cannot.

(65) *Anticausative passive*
    a. mado-garasu-ga (booto-ni-yotte) war-are-ta
       window-glass-Nom rioter-relying-on break-Pass-Past
       'The window glass was broken (by rioters).'

    Spontaneous
    b. mado-garasu-ga (*booto-ni-yotte) war-e-ta
       window-glass-Nom rioter-relying-on get-broken-Past
       'The window glass broke (*by rioters).'

A further piece of evidence is that a spontaneous sentence can have an NP marked by the instrumental postposition *de*, which denotes a natural cause of a change, while an anticausative passive cannot. This NP with *de* does not correspond to the subject of the active sentence.

(66) a. *kaze-ga   mado-garasu-o   wat-ta
       wind-Nom   window-glass-Acc   break-Past
       'The wind broke the window glass.'

Spontaneous
   b. mado-garasu-ga   kaze-de   war-e-ta
      window-glass-Nom   wind-Instr   get-broken-Past
      'The window glass broke because of the wind.'

Anticausative passive
   c. *mado-garasu-ga   kaze-de   war-are-ta
       window-glass-Nom   wind-Instr   get-Pass-Past
      'The window glass was broken because of the wind.'

(67) a. ?yuki-ga   densen-o   kit-ta
       snow-Nom   electric-wire-Acc   cut-Past
       'Snow cut the electric wire.'

Spontaneous
   b. densen-ga   yuki-de   kir-e-ta
      electric wire-Nom   snow-Instr   get-cut-Past
      'The electric wire got cut because of snow.'

Anticausative passive
   c. *densen-ga   yuki-de   kir-are-ta
       electric-wire-Nom   snow-Instr   cut-Pass-Past
      'The electric wire was cut because of snow.'

There is one subtle problem that has made a comprehensive study of the Japanese passive difficult. It is the case in which a single syntactic structure is ambiguous between the passive of interest and the anticausative passive. This happens when the subject of an anticausative passive is animate and the passive Agent is omitted.

(68) a. hahaoya-ga   kodomo-o   kuruma-kara   orosi-ta
       mother-Nom   child-Acc   car-Abl   take-down-Past
       'Mother took her child off the car.'

   b. kodomo-ga   kuruma-kara   oros-are-ta
      child-Nom   car-Abl   take-down-Pass-Past
      'The child was taken off the car.'
      'The child was subjected to being taken off the car.'

Sentence (68b) is ambiguous between two readings. One is a neutral description: someone took the child off the car. The other is adverse: the child was adversely affected by being taken off the car. Sentences like (68b) can disambiguated by two different kinds of agentive phrases.

(69) a. kodomo-ga   hahaoya-ni   kuruma-kara
        child-Nom   mother-Dat   car-Abl
        oros-are-ta
        take-down-Past
        'The child was subjected to his mother's taking him off the car.'

   b. kodomo-ga   hahaoya-ni-yotte   kuruma-kara
      child-Nom   mother-relying-on   car-Abl
      oros-are-ta
      take-down Past
      'The child was taken off the car by his mother.'

Sentence (69a) is a passive of interest and (69b) is an anticausative passive. *Kodomo* 'child' in (69a) is described as an entity that can be emotionally affected, while in (69b) the child is described as a physical entity that underwent a locational change. This is why (70a) is unacceptable. A corpse cannot be an emotionally affected entity.

(70) a. *kodomo-no nakigara-ga   hahaoya-ni
        child-Gen corpse-Nom   mother-Dat
        kuruma-kara   oros-are-ta
        car-Abl   take-down-Pass-Past
        'The child's corpse was subjected to its mother taking it off the car.'

   b. kodomo-no nakigara-ga   hahaoya-ni-yotte
      child-Gen corpse-Nom   mother-relying-on
      kuruma-kara   oros-are-ta
      car-Abl   take-down-Pass-Past
      'The child's corpse was taken off the car by its mother.'

In traditional Japanese grammar and in recent transformational approaches to the Japanese passive, sentences (69a) and (69b) fall into the category of the direct passive. However, our analysis has shown that the constructions that have been analyzed in terms of the direct passive are not semantically and syntactically homogeneous; they are divided into the passive of interest and the anticausative passive.

2.4 Attributive Passive

In this section, we will take a brief look at a third type of passive.

(71) a. John-ga   kono zassi-o   yoku   yomu
        John-Nom   this magazine-Acc   often   read
        'John often reads this magazine.'

THE PASSIVE IN JAPANESE 109

    b. *kono zassi-ga　　　　　　John-ni　yoku　　yom-are-ru
       this magazine-Nom　　　　John-Dat　often　read-Pass-Pres
       'This magazine is often read by John.'

(72) a. takusan-no wakamono-ga　　　　kono zassi-o　　　　yomu
        many-Gen young-people-Nom　this magazine-Acc　read
        'Many young people read this magazine.'

    b. kono zassi-ga　　　takusan-no wakamono-ni　　　yom-are-ru
      this magazine-Nom　many-Gen young-people-Dat　read-Pass-Pres
      'This magazine is read by many young people.'

(73) a. John-ga　　　kono tukue-o　　tukat-ta
        John-Nom　　this desk-Acc　use-Past
        'John used this desk.'

    b. *kono tukue-ga　　　John-ni　　tukaw-are-ta
      this desk-Nom　　　John-Dat　use-Pass-Past
      'This desk was used by John.'

(74) a. takusan-no yuumeizin-ga　　　　kono tukue-o　tukat-ta
        many-Gen big-name-person-Nom　this desk-Acc　use-Past
        'Many famous people used this desk.'

    b. kono tukue-ga　　takusan-no yuumeizin-ni　　　tukaw-are-ta
      this desk-Nom　　many-Gen big-name-person-Dat　use-Pass-Past
      'This desk was used by many famous people.'

(75) a. Chomsky-ga　　　kono ronbun-o　　yoku　　inyoosi-ta
        Chomsky-Nom　　this thesis-Acc　　often　　quote-Past
        'Chomsky often quoted this thesis.'

    b. kono ronbun-ga　　Chomsky-ni　　yoku　　inyoos-are-ta
      this thesis-Nom　　Chomsky-Dat　often　　quote-Pass-Past
      'This thesis was often quoted by Chomsky.'

(76) a. Chomsky-ga　　　kono syoosetu-o　yoku　　yon-da
        Chomsky-Nom　　this novel-Acc　　often　　read-Past
        'Chomsky often read this novel.'

    b. ?kono syoosetu-ga　Chomsky-ni　　yoku　　yom-are-ta
       this novel-Nom　　Chomsky-Dat　often　　read-Pass-Past
       'This novel was often read by Chomsky.'

Passive sentences with inanimate subjects like (72b), (74b), and (75b) are distinct from the anticausative passive in three ways. First, this type of passive is not restricted to factitive verbs. Second, these passive sentences have an agentive NP marked by dative *ni*. Third, these passive sentences are semantically static, while the anticausative passive is dynamic. This type of passive is allowed only when the rest of the sentence attributes some property to the participant denoted by the passive subject. Sentence (72b) entails 'this magazine is popular among young people'. In contrast, (71b) is unacceptable because the sentence can hardly be interpreted as attributing any property to the magazine. It is nonsensical to say 'this magazine is such that John reads it often'. As already pointed out, operative verbs normally cannot be passivized when the subject is inanimate, as in (73b). However, the passive sentence (74b), which has an operative verb and an inanimate subject, is acceptable because the rest of the sentence attributes a particular property to the subject NP *kono tukue* 'this desk'. Similarly, (75b) is acceptable because being quoted by one of the most famous linguists attributes a particular property to a linguistic thesis. However, being read by a prominent linguist is less likely to attribute a property to a novel. The analysis proposed above suggests that the condition under which this type of passive is acceptable is comparable to that for double-nominative constructions in Japanese. Both constructions are acceptable when the rest of the sentence attributes some property or condition to the participant denoted by the subject NP. In fact, this type of passive construction can also have two nominative NPs. Compare (75b) with (77).

(77)   kono ronbun-ga   dai-issyoo-ga   Chomsky-ni
       this thesis-Nom   the-first-chapter-Nom   Chomsky-Dat
       yoku   inyoos-are-ru
       often   quote-Pass-Past
       'This thesis—its first chapter is often quoted by Chomsky.'

Masuoka (1982) points out that the primary function of passive sentences like (72b), (74b), and (75b) is to foreground the direct object NP into the subject position. He claims that the most natural way to predicate an attribute of an entity is to put the entity in the position of the syntactic subject. The active sentence (75a), for instance, is not necessarily read as predicating an attribute of 'this thesis'. It can be interpreted as attributing an action to Chomsky. In contrast, (75b) explicitly ascribes an attribute to the thesis. It follows that the primary function of this type of passive is to foreground the direct object NP of an active sentence into the subject position in order to predicate an attribute of it. Recall that the primary function of the anticausative passive is to background the Agent denoted by the subject of the corresponding active sentence. These types of passives contrast in their primary functions.

2.5 Conclusion

The Japanese passive marked by *(r)are* is classified into three types: the passive of interest, the anticausative passive, and the attributive passive. The three types of passives have the following characteristics:

1. The passive of interest is obtained by introducing into the subject position a new participant from whose point of view the event is described. Therefore the subject needs to be animate, and typically human. This type of passive is semantically in opposition to the causative.

Active (S)
    →   Passive of interest: GET $(w, (S))$
    →   Permissive causative: LET $(w, (S))$
    →   Causative: CAUSE $(w, (S))$

2. The anticausative passive functions primarily to eliminate or background the causative Agent. The process is represented as follows:

CAUSE $(w, GO(w, y, z))$ → GO (x, y, z)

This type of passive is restricted mainly to factitive verbs.

3. The attributive passive functions primarily to foreground the direct object NP into subject position in order to predicate an attribute of it more explicitly. The semantic entailment of this type of passive is represented as follows:

BEcond (x, y)

We have claimed that the traditional distinction between direct and indirect passives is not sustainable either syntactically or semantically. The relation between the traditional distinction and our classification is shown in the following grid.

Indirect passive	
Direct passive	Passive of interest
	Anticausative passive
	Attributive passive

Chapter 5
Passive in Korean

1. Introduction

In this chapter we propose a semantics-based analysis of the passive in Korean.

It is widely accepted that Korean, like Japanese, has two types of passive, distinct both semantically and syntactically: the direct passive and the indirect passive (cf. Lee 1972).

(1) a. cangkwun-i cek-eykey cap-hi-essta
general-Nom enemy-Dat capture-Pass-Past
'The general was captured by the enemy.'
b. wuli-ka cek-eykey cangkwun-ul cap-hi-essta
we-Nom enemy-Dat general-Acc capture-Pass-Past
'We were subjected to the enemy's capturing our general.'

Indirect passive sentences like (1b) are syntactically distinct from direct passive sentences owing to the presence of an accusative NP. Semantically, subject affectedness, which is often adverse, is clearly recognized, while the direct passive is neutral in this respect. In the course of presenting a semantic and syntactic analysis of the passive in Korean, I reject the distinction between direct and indirect passives. I propose instead that the passive in Korean, like the passive in Japanese be reclassified into three types: the passive of interest, the anticausative passive, and the attributive passive.

The suffixes *i, ki, li, hi, u, chu, ku* are called voice suffixes. The first four share the vowel *i* and rest share *u*. In present-day Korean, the four suffixes with the vowel *i*, together with the suffix *u*, are used for both causative constructions and passive constructions, while the remaining two suffixes, *chu* and *ku*, are used as causative markers. Kim (1964) remarks that these suffixes were used mainly for the causative in Old Korean, and that their passive usage was merely a variation of their causative usage. The passive use has since been extended, but it is still under strong lexical restrictions. Selection of these suffixes by individual verbs is, in most cases, phonologically determined. However, the possibility of suffixation and the possibility of either the causative or the passive interpretation is to a considerable extent lexically conditioned. For instance, verbs that end with the vowel *i* do not have, in general, any voice suffix, for example, *ttayli* 'hit', *cikhi* 'defend', *tenci* 'throw'. Similarly, the transitive verbs derived by suffixation of *i, ki, li,* or *hi* tend to lack passive forms, for example, *cwuk-i* 'die-Cause → kill', *sal-li* 'live-Cause → make live, save', *wus-ki* 'laugh-Cause → make laugh'. However, this restriction is highly exceptional. For example, the verb *kki* 'put something between' has a passive form *kki-i* despite the final *i*. Both *mek-i* 'eat-Cause → feed' and *ip-hi* 'put on-Cause → make someone put on, clothe' have passive forms, *mek-i* and *ip-hi*.

2. Transitivization

The following intransitive verbs can be combined with a causative suffix to make corresponding transitive verbs.

nok 'melt'   →   nok-i 'make melt, melt'
cwul 'decrease'   →   cwul-i 'make decrease, decrease'
cwuk 'die'   →   cwuk-i 'make die, kill'
anc 'sit down'   →   anc-hi 'make sit down'
wus 'laugh'   →   wus-ki 'make laugh'
tha 'burn'   →   thay-wu 'make burn, burn'
mac 'fit, suit'   →   mac-chu 'make fit/suit'
tot 'rise up'   →   tot-ku 'make rise up'

These intransitive verbs indicate a spontaneous change. Although every change in the actual world has its cause, these verbs depict the process of the change itself.

(2) a. chel-i   nok-assta
       iron-Nom   melt-Past
       'The iron melted.'

   b. haksayng-swu-ka   cwul-essta
      student-number-Nom   decrease-Past
      'the number of students decreased.'

   c. kom-i   cwuk-essta
      bear-Nom   die-Past
      'A bear died.'

The thematic relations of these sentences are as follows:

(3) a. GOcond (IRON, SOLID, LIQUID)
   b. GOcond (THE NUMBER OF STUDENTS, y, LESS)
   c. GOcond (A BEAR, ALIVE, DEAD)

The verb *anc* 'sit down' typically has an animate subject and is ambiguous between an agentive reading of the subject and a nonagentive reading. The thematic relations of (4a), therefore, are represented as either (4b) or (4c).

(4) a. John-i   anc-assta
        John-Nom   sit-down-Past
        'John sat down.'

   b. GOcond (JOHN, y, SEATED)

   c. CAUSE (JOHN, GOcond (JOHN, y, SEATED))

The semantic representations of the sentences with the derived transitive verbs are obtained by embedding (3a, b, c) and (4b, c) into the causative pattern.

(5) a. John-i   chel-ul   nok-i-essta
        John-Nom   iron-Acc   melt-Cause-Past
        'John melted the iron.'

   b. CAUSE (JOHN, GOcond (IRON, SOLID, LIQUID))

(6) a. kukka-ka   haksayng-swu-lul   cwul-i-essta
        state-Nom   student-number-Acc   decrease-Cause-Past
        'The state decreased the number of students.'

   b. CAUSE (THE STATE, GOcond (THE NUMBER OF STUDENTS, y, LESS))

(7) a. John-i   kom-ul   cwuk-i-essta
        John-Nom   bear-Acc   die-Cause-Past
        'John killed a bear.'

   b. CAUSE (JOHN, GOcond (A BEAR, ALIVE, DEAD))

(8) a. Mary-ka   John-ul   anc-hi-essta
        Mary-Nom   John-Acc   sit-down-Cause-Past
        'Mary made John sit down.'

   b. CAUSE (MARY, GOcond (JOHN, y, SEATED))

   c. ?CAUSE (MARY, CAUSE (JOHN, GOcond (JOHN, y, SEATED)))

The semantic representation (8c) is a logical possibility, but when an NP occurs in the direct object position, it is not likely to be interpreted as an Agent. It follows that (8a) semantically contains (4a) with the reading (4b), rather than (4c)

We can set up a word derivational rule like (9) to derive transitive stems by means of the causative affixes. This transitivization is semantically represented as in (10).

(9)   Intransitive Stem + Causative {I}/{U} → Transitive Stem

({I} and {U} are the notations for the underlying morphemes representing *i, ki, li, hi,* and *u, chu, ku* respectively.)

(10) GO (*x, y, z*) → CAUSE (*w,* GO (*x, y, z*))

It may be worth pointing out at this stage that the semantic opposition in (10) corresponds to the relation obtaining between the two verbs that are most frequently used: *toy* 'become' and *ha* 'do'. The former is the most general verb of conditional change, and the latter the most general verb of causation. These two verbs, in combination with a noun or an adjective, form analytic predicates.

(11) a. John-i   kipp-ta
        John-Nom   happy-Pres
        'John is happy.'

     b. BEcond (JOHN, HAPPY)

(12) a. John-i   kipp-key   toy-essta
        John-Nom   happy-to   become-Past
        'John became happy.'

     b. GOcond (JOHN, *y*, HAPPY)

(13) a. Mary-ka   John-ul   kipp-key   ha-essta
        Mary-Nom   John-Acc   happy-to   do-Past
        'Mary made John happy.'

     b. CAUSE (MARY, GOcond (JOHN, *y*, HAPPY))

The examples in (12) and (13) suggest that the semantic opposition between the intransitive verbs and the transitive verbs examined above corresponds to the semantic opposition between *toy* 'become' and *ha* 'do'. In Chapter 3, we saw that the verb *toy* expresses two sets of thematic relations which are represented thus:

   a. GOcond (*x, y, z*)
   b. GOcond (*x*, NOT EXIST, EXIST)

It was pointed out that the double-nominative constructions with *toy* have the thematic relations in (b). However, when the verb *toy* is used with an adjective, as in (12a), it seems to express only the thematic relation (a), like English *become* and Japanese *naru*. This is clear from the presence of the particle *key*, which functions to mark an abstract Goal in (12a) and (13a). Compare the Japanese examples in (14) with the Korean ones in (15).

(14) *Positional*
　　a. John-ga　　gakkoo-ni　　it-ta
　　　　John-Nom　school-to　　go-Past
　　　　'John went to school.'

　　Possessional
　　b. John-ga　　Mary-ni　　hon-o　　age-ta
　　　　John-Nom　Mary-to　　book-Acc　give-Past
　　　　'John gave a book to Mary.'

　　Conditional
　　c. heya-ga　　kirei-ni　　nat-ta
　　　　room-Nom　clean-to　　become-Past
　　　　'The room became clean.'

(15) *Positional*
　　a. John-i　　hakkyo-ey　　ka-assta
　　　　John-Nom　school-to　　go-Past
　　　　'John went to school.'

　　Possessional
　　b. John-i　　Mary-eykey　chayk-ul　　cwu-essta
　　　　John-Nom　Mary-to　　book-Acc　　give-Past
　　　　'John gave a book to Mary.'

　　Conditional
　　c. pang-i　　kkaykkusha-key　　toy-essta
　　　　room-Nom　clean-to　　　　become-Past
　　　　'The room became clean.'

In the Japanese examples in (14), the Goal is marked by *ni* no matter how abstract the change expressed by the sentence is. In Korean, the Goal of a positional change is marked by *ey*, as in (15a); the Goal of a possessional change is marked by *eykey*, as in (15b); and that of a conditional change is marked by *key*, as in (15c). The Korean Dative postposition *eykey*, which is used as a marker for the Goal of a possessional change in (15b), consists of the locative Goal marker *ey* and the conditional Goal marker *key*. It was pointed out in Chapter 2 that the notion of possession is an intermediate level between the positional level and the most abstract conditional level. The form of *eykey*, which is typically used to mark the Goal of a possessional change, reflects this property of the notion of possession. When a change is conditional, as in (15c), and thus more abstract than a change of possession, the Goal marker loses *ey*, which marks concrete Goals.

We shall see later that *toy*, when used as a passive marker, also expresses the thematic relations GOcond (*x, y, z*) rather than GOcond (x, NOT EXIST, EXIST).

3. Intransitivization

Many transitive verbs, on being given a passive suffix, become intransitive verbs.

(16) tat 'close' → tat-hi 'be closed'
teph 'cover' → teph-hi 'be covered'
noh 'release' → noh-i 'be released'
mak 'stop up, block' → mak-hi 'be blocked'
ket 'collect' → ket-hi 'be collected'
an 'hold in one's arms, embrace' → an-ki 'be embraced'
ssis 'wash' → ssis-ki 'be washed'
cap 'catch' → cap-hi 'be caught'

Let us consider the following examples.

(17) a. John-i   mun-ul   tat-assta
John-Nom   door-Acc   close-Past
'John closed the door.'

a.' CAUSE (JOHN, GOcond (DOOR, OPEN, CLOSED))

b. mun-i   tat-hi-essta
door-Nom   close-Pass-Past
'The door closed.'

b.' GOcond (DOOR, OPEN, CLOSED)

(18) a. John-i   cepsi-lul   ssis-essta
John-Nom   dish-Acc   wash-Past
'John washed dishes.'

a.' CAUSE (JOHN, GOcond (DISHES, *y*, WASHED))

b. cepsi-ka   ssis-ki-essta
dish-Nom   wash-Pass-Past
'Dishes were washed.'

b.' GOcond (DISHES, *y*, WASHED)

The semantic structures of the (b) sentences in (17) and (18) are obtained by removing the causative pattern from the semantic structures of the (a) sentences. This suggests that these passives are identical with the spontaneous intransitive constructions in Japanese.[1] These passive sentences describe a change, represented by GO (x, y, z), without referring to an Agent. Therefore, this type of passive generally cannot have an Agent NP.

(19) cepsi-ka   *John-eykey/?John-eykey-uyhaye   ssis-ki-essta
dish-Nom   John-Dat/John-relying-on   wash-Pass-Past
'The dishes were washed by John.'

This intransitivization is restricted to factitive verbs. Verbs like *mek* 'eat' and *palp* 'tread on' cannot appear in passive sentences with an inanimate subject, like (17b) and (18b), even though they have passive forms *mek-hi* and *palp-hi*. This is because they are operative rather than factitive.

(20) a. John-i   ku sakwa-lul   mek-essta
John-Nom   the apple-Acc   eat-Past
'John ate the apple.'

b. *ku sakwa-ka   mek-hi-essta
the apple-Nom eat-Pass-Past
'The apple was eaten.'

(21) a. John-i   tol-ul   palp-assta
John-Nom   stone-Acc   tread-on-Past
'John trod on the stone.'

b. *tol-i   palp-hi-essta
stone-Nom   tread-on-Pass-Past
'The stone was trodden on.'

The verb *cap* 'catch, capture' can be used either as an operative verb denoting an action of 'seizing something', or a factitive verb standing for 'catching and possessing something'. Intransitivization is possible only in the latter reading.

(22) a. John-i   chayksang tali-lul   cap-assta
John-Nom   desk leg-Acc   seize-Past
'John grasped a leg of the desk.'

b. *chayksang tali-ka   cap-hi-essta
desk leg-Nom   seize-Pass-Past
'A leg of the desk was grasped.'

(23) a. John-i   manhun koki-lul   cap-assta
John-Nom   many fish-Acc   catch-Past
'John caught a lot of fish.'

b. manhun koki-lul   cap-hi-essta
many fish-Acc   catch-Pass-Past
'A lot of fish were caught.'

The word-derivational rule for this intransitivization is given in (24). This transitivization is semantically defined as anticausativization.

(24) Transitive stem + Passive {I}/{U} → Intransitive stem

(25) Causative → Anticausative
CAUSE (GO (x, y, z)) → GO (x, y, z)

Rule (24) and the semantic formalization in (25) clearly show that this intransitivization is exactly the reverse of the transitivization discussed in the previous section. We therefore may call the passive sentences cited in this section anticausative passives.

3.1 Auxiliary ci

Verbs like *kkay* 'break', *masu* 'destroy' and *cis* 'build' do not form intransitives by means of lexical derivation. Instead, the auxiliary *ci* is used to anticausativize these factitive verbs.

(26) a. John-i   changmun-ul   kkay-essta
       John-Nom   window-Acc   break-Past
       'John broke the window.'

   b. changmun-i   kkay-ci-essta
       window-Nom   break-Pass-Past
       'The window broke.'

(27) a. John-i   cip-ul   ci-essta
       John-Nom   house-Acc   build-Past
       'John built a house.'

   b. cip-i   cie-ci-essta
       house-Nom   build-Pass-Past
       'A house was built.'

The auxiliary *ci* indicates a conditional change interpretable as 'become', in many cases synonymous with the verb *toy* 'become'.

(28) a. i pang-i   kkaykkusha-kay   toy-essta
       this room-Nom   clean-to   become-Past
       'This room became clean.'

   b. i pang-i   kkaykkushay-ci-essta
       this room-Nom   clean-become-Past
       'This room became clean.'

Many transitive verbs have a *ci* form in addition to the intransitive forms derived by suffixation.

(29) a. mun-i   tat-hi-essta
       door-Nom   close-Pass-Past
       'The door closed.'

    b. mun-i   tata-ci-essta
       door-Nom   close-Pass-Past
       'The door was closed.'

Lee (1978) points out that an intransitive form like (29a) denotes a spontaneous change, while the *ci* form presupposes or implies the existence of a hidden Agent. He says that a change expressed by the *ci* form is the result intended by the unspecified Agent, while the intransitive forms have a strong implication that the change happened accidentally. He claims that the semantic difference between the two forms is manifest in the following examples.

(30) a. mun-i   cecello   tat-hi-essta
       door-Nom   of-its-own-accord   close-Pass-Past
       'The door closed of its own accord.'

    b. ?mun-i   cecello   tata-ci-essta
       door-Nom   of-its-own-accord   close-Pass-Past
       'The door was closed of its own accord.'

(31) a. yen-i   cenki-cwul-e   kel-li-essta
       kite-Nom   electric-wire-Loc   hang-Pass-Past
       'The kite was caught on an electric wire.'

    b. yen-i   cenki-cwul-e   kele-ci-essta
       kite-Nom   electric-wire-Loc   hang-Pass-Past
       'The kite was hung on an electric wire.'

Lee says that sentence (31b) indicates that the kite was hung on the wire deliberately, while it may have happened accidentally in (31a). Given Lee's analysis, the semantic difference between the intransitive form and the *ci* form can be described as a difference between process-orientation and agent-orientation. These two forms can be regarded as subtypes of the anticausative passive: the *ci* form presupposes the action of an unspecified Agent, while the intransitive form does not. The difference is also manifest in the fact that the *ci* form tolerates the presence of an Agent NP, marked by *ey-uyhaye* 'relying on' (comparable to Japanese *ni-yotte*) more easily than the intransitive form.

(32) a. ku cip-i   John-ey-uyhaye   cie-ci-essta
       the house-Nom   John-relying-on   build-Pass-Past
       'The house was built by John.'

    b. mun-i   John-ey-uyhaye   tata-ci-essta
       door-Nom   John-relying-on   close-Pass-Past
       'The door was closed by John.'

    c. *mun-i   John-ey-uyhaye   tat-hi-essta
       door-Nom   John-relying-on   close-Pass-Past
       'The door closed by John.'

Sentences (32a) and (32b) both sound a little unnatural, but (32c) sounds much more odd. It is often pointed out that this kind of passive sentence with an Agent NP is getting more and more frequent. The same is true for the Japanese anticausative passive.

When a verb does not have a lexically derived intransitive form, the *ci* form covers both process-oriented and agent-oriented functions.

(33) *Process-oriented*
    a. changmun-i   cecello   kkay-ci-essta
       window-Nom   of-its-own-accord   break-Pass-Past
       'The window broke of its own accord.'

    Agent-oriented
    b. changmun-i   John-ey-uyhaye   kkay-ci-essta
       window-Nom   John-relying-on   break-Pass-Past
       'The window was broken by John.'

3.2 Anticausative Passive of ha verbs

Korean, like Japanese, has an extremely productive word formation pattern consisting of an abstract NP + *ha* 'do'. The majority of abstract NPs taking part in this type of compound verb are of foreign origin, mainly Chinese.

    kensel-ha (construction-do) 'build, construct'
    phakoy-ha (destruction-do) 'destroy'
    paychi-ha (arrangement-do) 'arrange'
    chenday-ha (humiliation-do) 'humiliate'
    moyok-ha (insult-do) 'insult'
    ceyko-ha (rise-do) 'raise'

These compound verbs cannot combine with the voice suffixes. The voices of these verbs are distinguished by replacing *ha* 'do' with *sikhi* for the causative and *toy* 'become', *tangha* 'suffer', and *pat* 'receive' for the passive. The voice-marking system for *ha* compound verbs is as follows:

(34) Active
                    [___ ha] 'do'
→ Causative
                    [___ sikhi] 'make do'
→ Passive
                    [___ toy] 'become'
                    [___ tangha] 'suffer'
                    [___ pat] 'receive'

It has been pointed out that the semantic opposition between the active and the anticausative is represented by the opposition between *ha* 'do' and *toy* 'become'. Thus we may anticipate that the anticausative of *ha* compound verbs must be marked by *toy* 'become'. Passivization by *toy* in fact shows the characteristics that are inherent in the anticausative. First, passive verbs marked by *toy* allow inanimate subjects as well as animate ones, while passive verbs marked by the remaining two verbs do not, as we will see later.

(35) a. haksayng-tul-i   i cip-ul   kensel-ha-essta
        student-Pl-Nom   this house-Acc   build-Past
        'The student built this house.'

    b. i cip-i   (haksayng-tul-ey-uyhaye)   kensel-toy-essta
        this house-Nom   student-Pl-relying-on   build-Pass-Past
        'This house was built (by the students).'

(36) saynghwal swucwun-i   cecello   ceyko-toy-essta
     living standard-Nom   of-it-own-accord   raise-Pass-Past
     'The living standard rose of its own accord.'

It seems that the passive with *toy* is not specifically either process-oriented or agent-oriented. Sentence (35b) is semantically equivalent to an agent-oriented *ci* passive like (37a), while (36) is semantically equivalent to a simple intransitive sentence (37b), which is process-oriented.

(37) a. i cip-i   haksayng-tul-ey-uyhaye   cie-ci-essta
        this house-Nom   student-Pl-relying-on   build-Pass-Past
        'This house was built by the students.'

    b. saynghwal swucwun-i   cecello   oll-assta
        living standard-Nom   of-it-own-accord   rise-Past
        'The living standard rose of its own accord.'

Second, the passive with *toy*, like other anticausative passives, is basically restricted to factitive verbs. For instance, the semantic content of *moyok-ha* 'insult' does not fit into the factitive pattern represented by CAUSE (*w*, GO (*x, y, z*)) and, therefore, cannot take the *toy* passive form.

(38) a. Mary-ka John-ul moyok-ha-essta
Mary-Nom John-Acc insult-Past
'Mary insulted John.'

b. *John-i moyok-toy-essta
John-Nom insult-Pass-Past

The passive form with *toy* and the anticausative lexically derived passive can both take an agentlike NP marked by the dative *eykey* in some cases.

(39) *toy*-form
a. John-i kyengchal-ey-uyhaye/eykey choypho-toy-essta
John-Nom police-relying-on/Dat arrest-Pass-Past
'John was arrested by the police.'

Derived intransitive
b. John-i kyengchal-eykey cap-hi-essta
John-Nom police-Dat capture-Pass-Past
'John was arrested by the police.'

Kim (1964) claims that these dative NPs are oblique Agents. However, the dative *eykey*, like Japanese *ni*, is ambiguous: it marks either Goal or passive Agent. The NPs with *eykey* in (39a, b) can be interpreted simply as the Goals of the possessional changes represented in (40).

(40) GOposs (JOHN, *y*, POLICE)

When the subject of an active sentence is not Goal, the corresponding anticausative passive cannot have a dative NP, as is shown in (41) and (42).

(41) a. John-i cikwen-ul hayko-ha-essta
John-Nom worker-Acc dismiss-Past
'John dismissed the worker.'

a.' CAUSE (JOHN, GOcond (THE WORKER, WITH A JOB, WITHOUT A JOB))

b. cikwen-i (John-*eykey/ey-uyhaye) hayko-toy-essta
worker-Nom John-Dat/relying-on dismiss-Pass-Past
'The worker was fired (by John).'

b.' GOcond (THE WORKER, WITH A JOB, WITHOUT A JOB)

(42) a. cangkwun-i   ku puha-lul
       general-Nom   the subordinate-Acc
       censen-ey   phakyenha-essta
       the-front-to   send-Past
       'The general sent the subordinate to the front.'

   a.′ CAUSE (THE GENERAL, GOposit (THE SUBORDINATE, THE GENERAL, THE FRONT))

   b. ku puha-ka   (cangkwun-ey-uyhaye/*eykey)
      the subordinate-Nom   general-relying-on/Dat
      censen-ey   phakyen-toy-essta
      the-front-to send-Pass-Past
      'The subordinate was sent to the front (by the general).'

   b.′ GOposit (THE SUBORDINATE, y, THE FRONT)

The active subject in (41a) is simply Agent, and it is both Agent and Source in (42a). In these cases, the corresponding anticausative passives cannot have a dative NP corresponding to the subject NPs of the active counterparts. These facts indicate that the dative NPs in (39a) and (39b) can be plausibly regarded as Goals rather than Agents.

The various oppositions between the causative and the anticausative that are typically represented by the opposition between ha and *toy* is summarized as follows:

(43)   GO (x, y, z)   CAUSE (w, GO (x, y, z))

   a. toy 'become'   ha 'do' (lexical opposition)
   b. nok 'melt'   →   nok-i 'melt' (transitivization)
   c. ssis-ki 'be washed'   ←   ssis 'wash' (intransitivization)
   d. cie-ci 'be built'   ←   cis 'build' (*ci* form)
   e. kensel-toy 'be built'   ←   kensel-ha 'build' (*toy* form)

   Anticausative: (c), (d), (e)

4. Passive of Interest

Since the causative and the passive are marked by the same suffixes in Korean, many sentences are ambiguous between the causative and the passive. Sentence (44) allows three interpretations.

(44) cangkwun-i   puha-eykey   mal-koppi-lul
    general-Nom   subordinate-Dat   horse-bridle-Acc
    cap-hi-essta
    seize-Cause-Past
    'The general made/let the subordinate hold his horse's bridle.'
    'The general was subjected to the subordinate holding his horse's bridle.'

The first interpretation is that the *cangkwun* 'general' as Agent caused the event 'the subordinate held his horse's bridle'; the second is that the general did not prevent the event from taking place; the third is that he had no control over the event and was adversely affected as a consequence of it. Sentence (44) in the third interpretation is syntactically and semantically identical with the possessive reflexive type of the passive of interest in Japanese. The three interpretations share the event 'the subordinate held the bridle of the general's horse'. Therefore we assume that causative and passive sentences with structures identical to (44) are derived from active sentences like (45) by introducing a causative or permissive Agent and an Experiencer, respectively.

(45) puha-ka   cangkwun-uy   mal-koppi-lul   cap-essta
    subordinate-Nom general-Gen   horse-bridle-Acc seize-Past
    'The subordinate held the bridle of the general's horse.'

We assign the semantic structure (46) to (45) because the verb *cap* 'seize' is used as an operative verb here.

(46) SEIZE (THE SUBORDINATE, THE BRIDLE OF THE GENERAL'S HORSE)

If we symbolize the semantic structure in (46) as X, the three interpretations of (44) are represented as follows:

(47) a. CAUSE (THE GENERAL, (X))
    b. LET (THE GENERAL, (X))
    c. GET (THE GENERAL, (X))

The adoption of GET along with CAUSE and LET provides the full range of representations for ambiguous sentences like (44).

The causative and the passive of interest are not always ambiguous. The verb *mek* 'eat' has the distinct forms *mek-i* for the causative and *mek-hi* for the passive.

(48) a. Mary-ka   ku ai-eykey   pap-ul   mek-i-essta
       Mary-Nom   the child-Dat food-Acc   eat-Cause-Past
       'Mary made/let the child eat food.'

b. Mary-ka   pem-eykey   atul-ul   mek-hi-essta
      Mary-Nom   tiger-Dat   son-Acc   eat-Pass-Past
      'Mary was subjected to a tiger's eating her son.'

This type of passive, like the passive of interest in Japanese, is distinct from the anticausative passive discussed in the previous section in three ways. First, this type of passive is biased towards adverse affectedness, while the anticausative passive is neutral. The active sentence (45) does not entail that the general was adversely affected, while the passive sentence (44) does. Second, this type of passive does not allow an inanimate subject.

(49) a. John-i   chayksang   tali-lul   cap-essta
        John-Nom   desk   leg-Acc   seize-Past
        'John grasped a leg of the table.'
     b. *chayksang-i   John-eykey   tali-lul   cap-hi-essta
        desk-Nom   John-Dat   leg-Acc   seize-Pass-Past
        'The desk was subjected to John's grasping its leg.'

Third, this type of passive is not restricted to factitive verbs. As already pointed out, the verb *cap* can be used either as an operative verb denoting an action of 'seizing' or 'grasping', or as a factitive verb with a sense of 'capturing'. The anticausative passive is possible only in the latter sense, as we saw in (22) and (23). The passive of interest is possible with the former sense, as shown in (44). The verb *mek* 'eat', as shown in (20), cannot have the anticausative passive, while it can have the passive of interest, as in (48b). These facts indicate that the passive sentences (44) and (48b) have exactly the same characteristics as the possessive reflexive type of the passive of interest in Japanese. We have so far treated only so-called indirect passive sentences. However, it will be shown in the following discussion that the notions of indirect passive and passive of interest are not compatible, and that the division between the direct and the indirect passives does not capture the syntactic and semantic nature of the passive in Korean.

4.1 Passive Marking of ha Compound Verbs

When compound verbs with *ha* 'do' in active sentences appear in passive sentences containing accusative NPs, that is, in so-called indirect passive sentences, they take *tangha* 'suffer' or *pat* 'receive' in place of active *ha* 'do'. These passive forms are semantically in opposition to the causative *sikhi*.

(50) a. kyengchal-i   John-uy   atul-ul   choypho-ha-essta
        police-Nom   John-Gen   son-Acc   arrest-Past
        'The police arrested John's son.'

b. John-i   kyengchal-eykey   atul-ul
   John-Nom police-Dat   son-Acc
   choypho-sikhi-essta
   arrest-Cause-Past
   'John made/let the police arrest his son.'

c. John-i   kyengchal-eykey   atul-ul
   John-Nom police-Dat   son-Acc
   choypho-tangha-essta
   arrest-Pass-Past
   'John was subjected to the police's arresting his son.'

The passive marked by *pat* does not necessarily indicate that the subject is beneficially affected.

(51) kutul-i   cengbu-eykey   kwenli-lul
     they-Nom   government-Dat   rights-Acc
     tanap-pat-assta
     suppress-Pass-Past
     'They were subjected to the government's suppressing their rights.'

This type of passive cannot be marked by *toy* 'become' (see 52a), while the anticausative passive cannot be marked by *tangha* or *pat* (see 52b).

(52) a. *John-i   kyengchal-eykey   atul-ul
        John-Nom   police-Dat   son-Acc
        choypho-toy-essta
        arrest-Pass-Past
        'John was subjected to the police's arresting his son.'

     b. *i cip-i   haksayng-tul-ey-uyhaye
         this house-Nom   student-Pl-relying-on
         kensel-tangha/pat-essta
         build-Pass-Past
         'This house was built by students.'

The examples above indicate that *toy* 'become' is an anticausative passive marker, while *tangha* 'suffer' and *pat* 'receive' are markers of the passive of interest. What is important is that passive marking by *tangha* and *pat* is not restricted to the so-called indirect passive. The direct passive can also be marked by them, as in (53).

(53) a. kongcangcwu-ka   cikwen-tul-ul   hayko-ha-essta
        factory-owner-nom   worker-Pl-Acc   dismiss-Past
        'The factory owner dismissed the workers.'

Anticausative
b. cikwen-tul-i   (kongcangcwu-ey-uyhaye)
    worker-Pl-Nom   factory-owner-relying-on
    hayko-toy-essta
    dismiss-Pass-Past
    'The workers were dismissed (by the factory owner).'

c. cikwen-tul-i   kongcangcwu-eykey
    worker-Pl-Nom   factory-owner-Dat
    hayko-tangha-essta
    dismiss-Pass-Past
    'The workers were subjected to the factory owner's dismissing them.'

The passive sentence (53b), being an anticausative passive, is a neutral description of an event. The individuals denoted by the subject of (53c), in contrast, are described as persons who were adversely affected in consequence of the event. If a newscaster reported the event, he would likely choose (53b). If (53c) were chosen, it would give the impression that the newscaster was sympathetic to the workers.

Another piece of evidence for the analysis that the so-called direct passive is divided into the anticausative passive and the passive of interest is provided by passive sentences like (54a) and (54b).

(54) a. John-i   Mary-eykey   atul-ul   moyok-tangha-essta
         John-Nom   Mary-Dat   son-Acc   insult-Pass-Past
         'John was subjected to Mary's insulting his son.'

     b. John-i   Mary-eykey   moyok-tangha-essta
         John-Nom   Mary-Dat   insult-Pass-Past
         'John was subjected to Mary's insulting him.'

The verb *moyok-ha*, as a verb whose semantic content is not analyzable in terms of factitivity, cannot have the anticausative form marked by *toy*, as shown in (38). However, this verb can be passivized by *tangha*, as in (54). This suggests that the passive sentences (54a) and (54b), which are often characterized as an indirect passive sentence and a direct passive sentence, respectively, are best analyzed as examples of the passive of interest. As we did in the previous chapter, we admit two subtypes of the passive of interest: the complete reflexive type, like (53c) and (54b), and the possessive reflexive type, like (50c), (51), and (54a). The syntactic difference between the two subtypes is accounted for by a single deletion rule, shown in (55).

(55) a. John-i   [kyengchal-i   John-uy   atul-ul
        John-Nom   police-Nom   John-Gen   son-Acc
        choypho-]   tangha-essta
        arrest   Pass-Past

    → John-i   kyengchal-eykey   *(deleted)* atul-ul
        John-Nom   police-Dat   son-Acc
        choypho-tangha-essta
        arrest-Pass-Past

    'John was subjected to the police's arresting his son.'

   b. John-i   [kyengchal-i   John-ul
        John-Nom   police-Nom   John-Acc
        choypho-]   tangha-essta
        arrest   Pass-Past

    → John-i   kyengchal-eykey   *(deleted)*
        John-Nom   police-Dat
        choypho-tangha-essta
        arrest-Pass-Past

    'John was subjected to the police's arresting him.'

An anticausative passive sentence, as already pointed out, can have a dative NP when the subject of the corresponding active sentence is Goal. In this case, the anticausative sentence is formally very similar to the passive of interest, as exemplified below.

(56) *Anticausative*
   a. John-i   kyengchal-eykey   choypho-toy-essta
        John-Nom   police-Dat   arrest-Pass-Past
      'John was arrested by (to) the police.'

   a.' GOposs (JOHN, *y*, POLICE)

   Passive of interest
   b. John-i   kyengchal-eykey   choypho-tangha-essta
        John-Nom   police-Dat   arrest-Pass-Past
      'John was subjected to the police's arresting him.'

   b.' GET (JOHN (CAUSE (POLICE, GOposs (JOHN, *y*, POLICE))))

In passivizations of *ha* compound verbs, as in (56a) and (56b), the two types are still distinguished by the different passive markers. However, our analysis suggests the possibility that so-called direct passive sentences marked by voice suffixes, as in (57a), may be ambiguous between the readings of the anticausative passive and the passive of interest, represented in (57b) and (57c), respectively.

(57) a. John-i   kyengchal-eykey   cap-hi-essta
John-Nom   police-Dat   catch-Pass-Past
'John was arrested by (to) the police.'

b. GOposs (JOHN, y, POLICE)

c. GET (JOHN (CAUSE (POLICE, GOposs (JOHN, y, POLICE))))

The behavior of the suffix u seems to support this analysis. The passive suffixes *i, ki, li,* and *hi* have the possibility of being followed by another suffix u to yield a complex passive marker. Kim (1964:197) points out that this double suffixation is very frequently used in the northeastern area of Korea and is spreading to other dialects. One interesting fact is that this double suffixation has a more restricted distribution than that of single suffixation. First, double suffixation is blocked in passive sentences with inanimate subjects. The following anticausative passive sentences with inanimate subjects cannot have u.

(58) a. *cepsi-ka   ssis-ki-u-essta
     dish-Nom wash-Pass-Pass-Past
     'Dishes were washed.'
b. *mun-i   yel-li-u-essta
     door-Nom open-Pass-Pass-Past
     'The door opened.'

Passive sentences with animate subjects allow double suffixation, whether or not they have accusative NPs.

(59) a. John-i   kyengchal-eykey   cap-hi-u-essta
John-Nom   police-Dat   catch-Pass-Pass-Past
'John was subjected to the police's arresting him.'

b. John-i   kyengchal-eykey   atul-ul
John-Nom   police-Dat   son-Acc
cap-hi-u-essta
catch-Pass-Pass-Past
'John was subjected to the police's arresting his son.'

c. John-i   pem-eykey   pal-ul   mek-hi-u-essta
John-Nom   tiger-Dat   arm-Acc   eat-Pass-Pass-Past
'John was subjected to a tiger's eating his arm.'

When the subject is low in animacy, the passive sentence with *u* sounds odd. The passive sentence (23b), 'A lot of fish were caught', sounds strange if *u* is added to it, as in (60).

(60) ?manhun koki-ka   cap-hi-u-essta
     many fish-Nom   catch-Pass-Pass-Past
     'A lot of fish were caught.'

In (60), the 'fish' are described as emotionally affected by being caught.

The discussion above shows that *u* has the same distribution as *tangha* marking the passive of interest. From this we conclude that *u* inherently marks the passive of interest. The suffix *u* functions to disambiguate the passive of interest and the anticausative passive in cases like (57a). In (53), we saw that passive marking by *tangha* is not appropriate for the neutral reporting of a fact. Double suffixation is also inappropriate for the simple reporting of a fact.

(61) a. pemin-i   kyengchal-eykey   cap-hi-essta
        criminal-Nom   police-Dat   catch-Pass-Past
        'The criminal was arrested by the police.'
        'The criminal was subjected to the police arresting him.'

     b. pemin-i   kyengchal-eykey   cap-hi-u-essta
        criminal-Nom   police-Dat   catch-Pass-Pass-Past
        'The criminal was subjected to the police arresting him.'

Sentence (61b) is not appropriate for a newscaster's neutral reporting of the fact, while (61a) is.

We have so far pointed out that Korean, like Japanese, has two types of passive: the anticausative passive and the passive of interest. We also demonstrated that the semantic and syntactic nature of the passive in Korean cannot be captured by the traditional classification into the direct passive and the indirect passive. Moreover, some "direct passive" sentences with animate subjects are ambiguous between the anticausative passive and the passive of interest. The formal opposition between the anticausative passive and the passive of interest is represented as follows.

cap 'catch, capture'
    cap-hi *(Anticausative)*
    cap-hi (-u) *(Passive of interest)*

choypho-ha 'arrest'
    choypho-toy *(Anticausative)*
    choypho-tangha *(Passive of interest)*

We have admitted two subtypes of the passive of interest: the complete reflexive type and the possessive reflexive type. Japanese has a third type of the passive of interest: the nonreflexive type, as in (62).

(62) John-ga   sono kodomo-ni   nak-are-ta
     John-Nom   that child-Dat   cry-Pass-Past
     'John was subjected to the child's crying.'

This type of passive of interest is lacking in Korean. For example, (63) is interpreted only as a causative sentence.

(63) John-i   ku ai-eykey   wul-li-essta
     John-Nom   the child-Dat   cry-Cause-Past
     'John let the child cry.'

Thus we have:

(64) *Japanese Passive of interest*
     Complete reflexive type
     Possessive reflexive type
     Nonreflexive type

   Korean Passive of Interest
     Complete reflexive type
     Possessive reflexive type

5. Attributive Passive

Korean also has an attributive passive, exemplified in (65).

(65) a. John-i   i capci-lul   ilk-essta
        John-Nom   this magazine-Acc   read-Past
        'John read this magazine.'

     b. *i capci-ka   John-eykey   ilk-hi-essta
        this magazine-Nom   John-Dat   read-Pass-Past
        'This magazine was read by John.'

(66) a. manhun chengnyen-tul-i   i capci-lul   ilk-nunta
        many young-people-Pl-Nom   this magazine-Acc   read-Pres
        'Many young people read this magazine.'

     b. i capci-ka   manhun chengnyen-tul-eykey   ilk-hi-nta
        this magazine-Nom   many young-people-Pl-Dat   read-Pass-Past
        'This magazine is read by many young people.'

This type of passive, like the attributive passive in Japanese, is allowed only when the rest of the sentence attributes some property to the participant denoted by the subject. The primary function of this type, as pointed out in the previous chapter, is to foreground the direct object NP in the subject position in order to make the predication of its attribute more natural.

We have so far confirmed that our analysis of the Japanese passive applies well to the Korean passive. The two languages have three types of passives that are syntactically and semantically parallel. The two languages differ, as far as the passive is concerned, only in that Korean does not have the nonreflexive type of the passive of interest, and that passivization in Korean is more lexically conditioned.

Chapter 6
Some Typological Observations on Passives and Dative-Shift

This chapter compares the passive in English and the passive of interest in Korean and Japanese in relation to the phenomenon of Dative-shift.

Within Relational Grammar, it is claimed that direct objects and only direct objects can become subjects of passive sentences. According to the universals of passivization proposed by Perlmutter and Postal (1977), also adopted by Bresnan (1981b), the passive is derived by promoting the direct object of an active clause to the subject of a passive clause while the original subject loses its grammatical relation, as we saw in Chapter 4. In English, the indirect object is assumed to be promoted to direct object via Dative-shift before being promoted to the subject of a passive clause, as shown in (1).

(1) a. John gave a book to *Mary*. (IO)
    b. John gave *Mary* a book. (DO)
    c. *Mary* was given a book. (Subj)

Sometimes the term "Dative-shift" is used in a broader functional sense to explain the relation between such sentences as (2a) and (2b).

(2) a. Mary hit *John's* face.
    b. Mary hit *John* in the face. (DO)
    c. *John* was hit in the face. (Subj)

Thus, passivization in English is often accounted for in connection with Dative-shift. From the semantic viewpoint, Dative-shift and passivization in English seem to depend on the fact that the participant to whom the action is directed is "affected." 'Giving a book to Mary' in (1) necessarily entails 'causing Mary to have a book', and 'hitting John's face' necessarily entails 'hitting John' because of the inalienable relation between 'John' and 'his face'. These necessary entailments can be formalized as in (3) according to our analysis proposed in Chapter 2.

(3) a. CAUSE (JOHN, GOposs (A BOOK, JOHN, MARY))
       → CAUSE (JOHN, GOcond (MARY, y, WITH A BOOK))

    b. HIT (MARY, JOHN'S FACE)   →   HIT (MARY, JOHN)

This type of affectedness, involving the participant to whom the action is directed, was called "objective affectedness" in Chapter 4.

An analog of the Dative-shift in Korean, as described in Chapter 2, is double-accusativization. Double-accusativization, like Dative-shift in English, depends on the semantic notion of objective affectedness.

(4) a. emeni-ka   ai-eykey/lul   yak-ul   mek-i-essta
       mother-Nom   child-Dat/Acc   medicine-Acc   eat-Cause-Past
       'Mother gave {medicine to her child / her child medicine}.'

   b. John-i   ai-uy/lul   son-ul   cap-essta
      John-Nom   child-Gen/Acc   hand-Acc   catch-Past
      'John grasped {the child's hand / the child by the hand}.'

   c. cek-i   John-uy/*ul   atul-ul   salhayha-essta
      enemy-Nom   John-Gen/Acc   son-Acc   slaughter-Past
      'The enemy slaughtered John's son.'

Double-accusativization is allowed in (4a) and (4b) because both sentences mean that the subject NP took an action aimed at affecting the referent of the NP that is optionally accusativized. Sentence (4c) cannot be double-accusativized since it does not necessarily mean that 'the enemy intended to affect John' or that the action taken by 'the enemy' was directed at 'John'. However, one potentially serious problem for the universal characterization proposed by Permutter and Postal is that sentence (4c), as well as (4a) and (4b), can be passivized in spite of being unable to appear in the double-accusative form.

(5) a. ai-ka   emeni-eykey   yak-ul   mek-hi-essta
       child-Nom   mother-Dat   medicine-Acc   eat-Pass-Past
       'The child was subjected to his mother giving him medicine.'

   b. ai-ka   John-eykey   son-ul   cap-hi-essta
      child-Nom   John-Dat   hand-Acc   catch-Pass-Past
      'The child was subjected to John's grasping his hand.'

   c. John-i   cek-eykey   atul-ul   salhay-tangha-essta
      John-Nom   enemy-Dat   son-Acc   slaughter-Pass-Past
      'John was subjected to the enemy's slaughtering his son.'

Passivization in Korean has often been explained on the basis of double-accusativization (Kim 1964, Sung 1976): the indirect object or the possessor NP becomes the direct object by taking the accusative marker and then becomes the subject of a passive sentence. This analysis is compatible with the characterization of passivization in Relational Grammar. However, passive sentences like (5c) are serious counterexamples to the attempt to account for the passive in Korean on the basis of double-accusativization.

In Chapter 4, we pointed out that in Japanese, in addition to transitive verbs, intransitive verbs which do not express any intentionality on the part of the subject can also be passivized.

(6) a. ame-ga   hut-ta
      rain-Nom   fall-Past
      'It rained.'

    b. John-ga   ame-ni   hur-are-ta
      John-Nom   rain-Dat   fall-Pass-Past
      'John was rained on.'

Examples (5c) and (6b) show that the passivization in Korean and Japanese is independent of the active subject's intentionality and the directedness of the action or event, and also independent of direct-objecthood. The passive sentences (5c) and (6b) mean that the subject NPs are emotionally affected as a consequence of events that were not directed at them. We defined this type of passive as the "passive of interest" because it is used when the speaker describes an event from the viewpoint of a particular individual's concerns. We argued earlier on that the affectedness expressed in these passive sentences may be called "empathy-based affectedness." The relation between an event and objective affectedness was described as a cause–effect relation, and the relation between an event and empathy-based affectedness was described, in logical terms, as a reason–effect relation. The cause is a necessary and sufficient condition for producing the effect, while the reason may be no more than a necessary condition for producing the effect.

We have so far pointed out that, in English, Dative-shift and the passive both depend on the semantic notion of objective affectedness while, in Korean, Dative-shift depends on objective affectedness and the passive of interest depends on empathy-based affectedness. The difference between English and Korean is shown in (7).

(7) *English*
      Dative-shift   Objective affectedness
      Passive   Objective affectedness

    Korean
      Dative-shift   Objective affectedness
      Passive   Empathy-based affectedness

It seems that the characterization of the passive in terms of direct-objecthood applies only to those languages whose passive depends semantically on objective affectedness.

It is interesting to note that the notion of empathy-based affectedness used to be relevant to the English dative. Earlier English had a so-called "ethical dative" (Curme 1931) or "emotional indirect object" (Jespersen 1961), exemplified in (8).

(8) a. Why, he would slip *you* out of this chocolate-house.
    b. Whip *me* such honest knaves.

During the period when English had the ethical dative, the NPs preceded by the preposition *on* in (9) were expressed by the simple dative form. The use of *on* is a later development.

(9) a. The fire has gone out on me.
    b. He has gone back on me.
    c. My son died on me.

In (9a), the event *the fire has gone out* seems to be best regarded as the reason for my being affected rather than the cause. It is plausible to assume, then, that at an earlier period the notion of objective affectedness was subsumed under empathy-based affectedness, just as the cause-effect relation is logically included in the reason–effect relation. It follows that English, as far as the dative is concerned, has changed from a language in which the reason–effect relation is relevant, to one that mainly expresses the cause–effect relation. Without this historical change specific to English, Dative-shift and the passive could hardly have been correlated. The discussion so far shows that Dative-shift and passivization should be regarded as two grammatical processes which are, in principle, independent of each other.

Syntactically, passivization has been analyzed as intransitivization (Perlmutter and Postal 1977), a process that decreases the number of arguments taken by a predicate: $P_{n+1} \rightarrow P_n$ (Keenan 1980, 1985). In my view, this is the syntactic characterization of one type of passive, namely the passive depending on the notion of objective affectedness. The other type of passive, the one depending on empathy-based affectedness is, on the contrary, characterized as a process of introducing a new argument. For instance, the passive subject *John* in (6b) never appears as an argument taken by the corresponding active verb. This type of passive, like the ethical dative, is used when the speaker describes an event not from a neutral viewpoint, but in terms of the interest of somebody who may or, more typically, may not be directly involved in the event denoted by the verb.

This indirect participant is naturally expressed as a new argument which is outside the scope of the transitivity of the verb, and is appended to the sentence as a whole. Characterizing the passive and the ethical dative as processes of introducing a new argument related to the sentence as a whole also explains a property common to the passive of interest in Japanese and the English ethical dative, namely that they are independent of whether the verb is transitive or intransitive. This characterization also provides some account of the formal similarity between the passive and the causative in Korean and Japanese, and even in English. We have seen that the passive and the causative in Korean and Japanese are formally very similar. In English, what semantically corresponds to the ethical dative is not the ordinary *be*-passive, but the so-called "passive of experience," as in (10). Sentence (10b), like some Korean passive sentences, is ambiguous between the passive and the causative.

(10) a. I had my son die.
b. I had the door shut.

The formal similarity between the causative and the passive that depends on empathy-based affectedness may be attributed to the fact that they are both characterized as processes of introducing a new argument.

The following three points summarize our conclusions.

1. The notion of affectedness is divided into two types: objective affectedness and empathy-based affectedness. The former corresponds logically to the cause–effect relation, while the latter corresponds to the reason–effect relation.

2. The two types of affectedness correspond to two types of passives that are represented by the *be*-passive in English and the passive of interest in Japanese and Korean, respectively.

3. The passive that depends on objective affectedness is characterized syntactically by a decrease in the number of arguments in the clause, while the passive that depends on empathy-based affectedness is characterized by the introduction of a new argument.

Notes

Chapter 1

1. Jackendoff (1983, 1987) proposes an elaborate framework of thematic relations. The new framework introduces such entities as Thing, Event, State, Action, Place, Path, Property, and Amount. These basic categories are expanded into more complex expressions by such formation rules as the following.

   (1)   a. PLACE → [$_{Place}$ PLACE-FUNCTION (THING)]

   b. PATH → $\begin{bmatrix} _{Path} \begin{Bmatrix} \text{TO} \\ \text{FROM} \\ \text{TOWARD} \\ \text{AWAY-FROM} \\ \text{VIA} \end{Bmatrix} \left(\begin{Bmatrix} \text{THING} \\ \text{PLACE} \end{Bmatrix} \right) \end{bmatrix}$

   c. EVENT → $\begin{Bmatrix} [_{Event} \text{ GO (THING, PATH)}] \\ [_{Event} \text{ STAY (THING, PLACE)}] \end{Bmatrix}$

   d. STATE → $\begin{Bmatrix} [_{State} \text{ BE (THING, PLACE)}] \\ [_{State} \text{ ORIENT (THING, PATH)}] \end{Bmatrix}$ (Jackendoff 1987:375)

   Source and Goal, which are treated in Jackendoff (1976) as the second and the third arguments of the function GO (x, y, z), are now replaced by the notion of Path, which has an internal structure with Place. Thus, the semantic structure of 'John ran into the room' is represented as (2).

   (2)   [$_{Event}$ GO ([$_{Thing}$ JOHN], [$_{Path}$ TO ([$_{Place}$ IN ([$_{Thing}$ ROOM])])])]

   The new framework provides us with more adequate ways of formalizing semantic structures of sentences. For example, the difference between the semantic structures of (3a) and (3b) can now be represented formally, whereas in the former framework it cannot.

   (3)   a. John ran to the house.
            [$_{Path}$ TO [$_{Place}$ HOUSE]]

         b. John ran toward the house.
            [$_{Path}$ TOWARD [$_{Place}$ HOUSE]]

   In the following chapters, however, the simplified formalization proposed by Jackendoff (1976) will be used since it seems sufficient for our purposes. The primary purpose of this book is not to develop the formalization itself. What is important is that all the deficiencies of the theory of thematic relations proposed by Gruber and Jackendoff (1972, 1976) that will be discussed in the following sections are shared by Jackendoff (1983, 1987).

2. Noticing the deficiency of his theory of thematic relations, Jackendoff (1987) proposes to add the "action" tier to the thematic tiers. This modification is motivated by the analysis of operative sentences like (1).

(1) Sue hit Fred.

In (1), "the thing in motion" is Sue or, more precisely, Sue's hand, while the thing affected is Fred. Jackendoff assigns Theme to the former and Patient to the latter. Such a distinction has been missing from the theory of thematic relations. A test for the Patient role is the ability of an NP to appear in the frame (2).

(2) {What happened/What y did} to NP was ...

Now semantic roles fall into two tiers: a thematic tier dealing with motion and location, and an action tier dealing with Agent–Patient relations. The semantic structure of (3a) is represented as (3b).

(3) a. Bill rolled the ball down the hill

b. $$\begin{bmatrix} \text{CAUSE} & ([\text{BILL}], [\text{GO }([\text{BALL}], [\text{DOWN }([\text{HILL}])])]) \\ \begin{bmatrix} \text{ACT} \\ \text{VOL} \end{bmatrix} & ([\text{BILL}], [\text{BALL}]) \end{bmatrix}$$

This representation reads that the ball is Theme in the thematic tier and Patient in the action tier. Jackendoff also says that the role Patient tends to be associated with direct object position, just as Agent is associated with subject position.

However, this new proposal is highly speculative, as Jackendoff himself admits, and cannot escape from criticisms made in the preceding sections. First, his framework is still not able to account for the semantic differences among the following sentences.

(4) a. John drained water from the pool.
    b. John drained the pool of water.
    c. *John drained water from the pool empty.
    d. John drained the pool empty of water.
    e. John drained the pool.

In his theory, *water* in (4a) is Theme and Patient, while *the pool* in (4b) is only Patient. Then, is *the pool* in (4d) and (4e) only Patient? This seems totally counterintuitive. Sentences (4d) and (4e) are semantically about the conditional change undergone by *the pool* rather than the locational change undergone by *water*. This is why the Goal of the conditional change can be specified in (4d) while it cannot in (4c).

Also, no one would like to say that (5) is about a motion of a broken arm from Mary to John. However this is the only possible interpretation in Jackendoff's theory since a broken arm is assigned the role Theme.

(5) Mary gave John a broken arm.

These problems came from the fact that he does not allow each verb to have more than one set of thematic relations and his modification is not based upon an adequate characterization of the meaning of verbs.

3. The term "condition" is adopted from Ikegami (1975). It covers three distinct semantic parameters proposed by Jackendoff: The identificational, existential, and circumstantial.

4. The term "ambivalent verbs" is from Lyons (1977). In his analysis, verbs like *kill* and *break* are described as being ambivalent, that is, operative–factitive. However, one can say *John killed Mary* in a situation where John did not directly operate upon Mary, for example, by giving her poison or not giving her any food for a long time. Therefore, these verbs are treated here simply as factitive verbs.

Chapter 2

1. By "Dative-shift," we mean the shift or promotion of an argument from an oblique position to direct object. Therefore it includes traditional Dative advancement and Possessor ascension. See Givón (1990, chapters 6 and 17) for similar use.

2. There is a group of verbs that our semantics cannot account for, verbs like *donate, report,* and *construct*. The following examples are from Gropen et al. (1989).

> John told/reported the news to Bill.
> John told/*reported Bill the news.
>
> Kate showed/demonstrated the technique to Alan.
> Kate showed/*demonstrated Alan the technique.
>
> Debbie built/constructed a cradle for Ezra.
> Debbie built/*constructed Ezra a cradle.
>
> Max got/obtained a ticket for Alice.
> Max got/*obtained Alice a ticket.

Gropen (1989) makes a plausible claim that the Dative-shift is constrained not only semantically but also morphologically. They say that Dative-shift verbs must belong to the native-stem class rather than to the Latinate class. They hypothesize that children, when they learn English, generalize the semantic rule of Dative-shift only to the native-stem class. Although children are insensitive to the etymology of the words, the distinction between Latinate and native vocabulary can be recast in morphological or phonological terms. Many Latinate stems could be those formed by combinations of a finite list of designated meaningless morphemes such as *per, con, mit, sume*, and so on, while the native class could be defined in phonological terms, with its verbs being monosyllabic or polysyllabic with initial stress. If we adopt this claim, our definition should be modified as follows: Dative-shift is a semantically motivated, but morphologically constrained process.

Chapter 5

1. In Chapter 4, the Japanese intransitive constructions comparable to this type of Korean "passive" were referred to simply as "spontaneous" constructions. Whether or not to use the term "passive" seems to be almost a terminological matter. However, there is one reason for using the term "passive" here. That is the fact that these intransitivizers are also used as markers for other types of passive in Korean.

References

Allerton, D. J. 1978. Generating indirect objects in English. *Journal of Linguistics* 14:21–33.

Allwood, J., L. G. Anderson, and Osten Dahl. 1977. *Logic in linguistics.* Oxford: Oxford University Press.

Anderson, J. M. 1971. *The grammar of case: Toward a localistic theory.* Cambridge: Cambridge University Press.

Anderson, R. S. 1977. Comments on the Paper by Wasow. In *Formal syntax,* ed. by P. Culicover, T. Wasow, and A. Akmajian. New York: Academic Press.

Auwera, J. V. D. 1981. *What do we talk about when we talk? Speculative grammar and the semantic and pragmatic focus.* Amsterdam: John Benjamins.

Bach, E. W. 1980. In defence of passive. *Linguistics and Philosophy* 3:397–341.

Barber, E. J. W. 1980. Voice: Beyond the passive. *Berkeley Linguistic Society* 1:16–24.

Barnes, B. K. 1985. A functional explanation of French nonlexical datives. *Studies in Language* 92:159–195.

Beedham, C. 1981. The passive in English, German and Russian. *Journal of Linguistics* 17:319–326.

Bennett, D. C. 1981. *Spatial and temporal uses of English prepositions: An essay in stratificational semantics.* New York: Longman.

Bolinger, Dwight. 1975. *Aspects of language,* 2nd ed. New York: Harcourt Brace Jovanovich.

Bresnan, Joan. 1978. A realistic transformational grammar. In *Linguistic theory and psychological reality,* ed. by M. Halle, J. Bresnan, and G. Miller. Cambridge, Mass.: MIT press.

———. 1981a. Poliadicity: Part 1 of theory of lexical rules and representations. In *Lexical grammar,* ed. by T. Hoekstra, H. van der Hulst and M. Moortgat. Dordrecht: Foris.

———. 1981b. The passive in lexical theory. In *The mental representation of grammatical relations,* ed. by J. Bresnan, pp. 3–86. Cambridge, Mass.: MIT Press.

Channon, R. 1982. 3-2 advancement, beneficiary advancement, and with. *Berkeley Linguistic Society* 8:271–282.

Chappell, H. 1980. Is the get-passive adversative? *Papers in Linguistics* 13:411–452.

Chomsky, Noam. *Lectures on government and binding.* Dordrecht: Foris.

Chung, Sandra. 1981. An object-creating rule in Bahasa Indonesia. *Linguistic Inquiry* 7:41–87.

Comrie, Bernard. 1977. In defence of spontaneous demotion: The impersonal passive. In *Syntax and semantics* 8, *Grammatical relations,* ed. by Peter Cole and Jerrold M. Sadock, pp. 47–58. New York: Academic Press.

———. 1983. *Language universals and linguistic typology.* Basil Blackwell.

Culicover, P., T. Wasow, and A. Akmajian. 1977. *Formal syntax.* New York: Academic Press.

Curme, George O. 1931. *Syntax.* Boston: D. C. Heath.

Davidson, Alice. 1980. Peculiar passive. *Language* 56:42–66.

Dik, S. C., ed. 1984. *Advances in functional grammar.* Dordrecht: Foris.

Dowty, David. 1979. *Word meaning and Montague grammar.* Dordrecht: Reidel.

Dubinsky, S. 1985. Oblique to direct object advancement in Japanese. *Linguistic Analysis* 15:57–75.

Erteschik-Shir, N. 1979. Discourse constraints on dative movement. In *Syntax and semantics* 12, *Discourse and syntax,* ed. by Talmy Givón. New York: Academic Press.

Falts, L. M. 1978. On indirect objects in universal syntax. *Chicago Linguistic Society* 14:76–87.

Farmer, A. K. 1984. *Modularity in syntax: A study in Japanese and English.* Cambridge, Mass.: MIT Press.

Fillmore, Charles. 1968a. The case for case. In *Universals in linguistic theory,* ed. by Emmon Bach and Robert T. Harms, pp. 1–88. New York: Holt, Reinhart and Winston.

———. 1968. Lexical entries for verbs. *Foundations of Language* 4:373–393.

———. 1970. The grammar of "hitting" and "breaking." In *Readings in English transformational grammar,* ed. by R. A. Jacobs and P. S. Rosenbaum, pp. 120–133. Waltham, Mass.: Ginn and Co.

———. 1977. The case for case reopened. In *Syntax and semantics* 8, *Grammatical relations,* ed. by Peter Cole and Jerrold M. Sadock, pp. 59–82. New York: Academic Press.

Foley, A. William, and Robert D. Van Valin. 1984. *Functional syntax and universal grammar.* Cambridge: Cambridge University Press.

———. 1985. Information packaging in the clause. In *Language typology and syntactic description: Clause structure,* ed. by T. Shopen pp. 282–314. Cambridge: Cambridge University Press.

Fodor, Janet D. 1977. *Semantics: Theories of meaning in generative grammar.* New York: Crowell.

Fox, B. 1981. Body part syntax: Toward a universal characterization. *Studies in Linguistics* 5:324–342.

Gim, Cha-gyun. 1980. Kwuke uy sayek kwa swutong uy uymi. *Hankul* 168:3–47.

Givón, Talmy. 1979. *On understanding grammar.* New York: Academic Press.

———. 1990. *Syntax: A functional typological introduction.* 2 vols. Amsterdam: John Benjamins.

Green, Georgia M. 1974. *Semantics and syntactic regularity.* Bloomington: Indiana University Press.
Gropen, Jess, S. Pinker, M. Hollander, R. Goldberg, and R. Wilson. 1989. The learnability and acquisition of the dative alternation in English. *Language* 65:203–258.
Gruber, J. 1965. Studies in lexical relations. Ph. D. dissertation, Massachusetts Institute of Technology.
———. 1976. *Lexical structure in syntax and semantics.* North-Holland Linguistic Series 25. Amsterdam: North-Holland.
Grunau, J. J. M. 1985. Towards a systematic theory of the semantic role inventory. *Chicago Linguistic Society* 21(1):144–159.
Haegeman, L. 1985. The get-passive and Burzio's generalization. *Lingua* 66:53–77.
Halliday, M. A. K. 1967. Notes on transitivity and theme in English. *Journal of Linguistics* 3:201–237.
———. 1968. Notes on transitivity and theme in English. *Journal of Linguistics* 4:179–215.
Hashimoto, S. 1959. *Kokubunpoo taikeiron.* Tokyo: Iwanami.
Hawkins, R. 1979. On "Generating indirect objects in English": A reply to Allerton. *Journal of Linguistics* 17:1–9.
Hoekstra, T. 1984. *Transitivity: Grammatical relations in government-binding theory.* Dordrecht: Foris.
Hopper, Paul J. 1985. Causes and effects. *Chicago Linguistic Society* 21:67–88.
Howard, Irwin, and Agnes M. Niyekawa-Howard. 1976. Passivization. In *Syntax and semantics 5, Japanese generative grammar,* ed. by Masayoshi Shibatani, pp. 201–237. New York: Academic Press.
Ikegami, Y. 1975. *Imiron.* Tokyo: Taishukan.
———. 1981a. *Suru to naru no gengogaku.* Tokyo: Taishukan.
———. 1981b. "Activity," "Accomplishments" "Achievement": A language that can't say "I burned it, but it didn't burn" and one that can. *Linguistic Agency* 1–24 (University of Trier).
———. 1982a. Source vs. Goal: A case of linguistic dissymmetry. In *Language and cognitive styles,* ed. by R. St. Clair and W. von Raffler-Engle, pp. 1–24. Lisse: Swets and Zeitlinger.
———. 1982b. Indirect causation and de-agentivization: The semantics of involvement in English and Japanese. *Tokyo Daigaku Kyooyoo Gakubu Kenkyuu Kiyoo* 29:95–112.
Im, H. B. 1983. Kwuke phitonghwa uy tongsa wa uymi. In *Kwuke uy thongsa uymilon,* ed. by Y. K. Ko and K. S. Nam, pp. 28–47. Seoul: Tab Chulpansa.
Inoue, K. 1976. *Henkei bunpoo to nihongo.* Tokyo: Taishukan.
———. 1983. *Nihongo no kihon koozoo.* Tokyo: Sanseido.
Izui, H. 1967. *Gengo no koozoo.* Tokyo: Kinokuniya Shoten.
———. 1970. Ditopical expressions in Japanese and other languages. In *Gengo no sekai,* pp. 427–430. Tokyo: Tsukuma Shobo.

Jackendoff, R. 1972. *Semantic interpretation in generative grammar*. Cambridge, Mass.: MIT Press.
——. 1976. Toward an explanatory semantic representation. *Linguistic Inquiry* 7:89–150.
——. 1983. *Semantics and cognition*. Cambridge, Mass.: MIT Press.
——. 1987. The status of thematic relations in linguistic theory. *Linguistic Inquiry* 16:369–412.
Jacobsen, W. 1982. The semantics of spontaneity in Japanese. *Berkeley Linguistic Society* 7:104–115.
Jesperson, Otto. 1961. *A modern English grammar*, part 3. Copenhagen: Munksgaad; London: Allen and Unwin.
Kayne, R. S. 1984. *Connectedness and binary branching*. Dordrecht: Foris.
Keenan, Edward L. Some universals of passive in relational grammar. *Chicago Linguistic Society* 11:340–352.
——. 1980. Passive is phrasal, not sentential or lexical. In *Lexical grammar*, ed. by T. Hoekstra, H. van der Hulst, and M. Moortgat. Dordrecht: Foris.
——. 1985. Passive in the world's languages. In *Language typology and syntactic description*, ed. by T. Shopen, pp. 243–281. Cambridge: Cambridge University Press.
Kim, Han-kon. 1983. Ilunpa "-i" sayek, phitong uy hwayongloncek coken. *Hankul* 180:35–51.
Kim, P. H. 1964. *Cosene tongsa hyengyongsa uy sang*. Pyongyang: Kwahagwon Press.
Kim, Y. H. 1978. Kyepcwuelon. *Hankul* 162:37–73.
Kitahara, Y. 1984. *Nihon bunpoo no shooten*. Tokyo: Kyoiku Shuppan.
Klaiman, M. H. 1982a. Toward a universal semantics of indirect subject constructions. *Berkeley Linguistic Society* 17:123–135.
——. 1982b. Affectedness and the voice system of Japanese. *Berkeley Linguistic Society* 18:398–413.
——. 1982c. Defending "voice": Evidence from Tamil. *Chicago Linguistic Society* 18:267–281.
Kuno, Susumu, and E. Kaburaki. 1977. Empathy and syntax. *Linguistic Inquiry* 8:627–672.
Kuno, Susumu. *The structure of the Japanese language*. Cambridge, Mass.: MIT Press.
Kuroda, S.-Y. 1965. Generative grammatical studies in the Japanese language. Ph.D. dissertation, Massachusetts Institute of Technology.
——. 1980. Bun koozoo no hikaku. In *Nichi-eigo hikaku kooza*, vol. 2, *Bunpoo*, ed. by T. Kunihiro, pp. 23–62. Tokyo: Taishukan.
Lakoff, R. 1971. Passive resistance. *Chicago Linguistic Society* 7:149–162.
Larson, R. K. 1988. On the double object construction. *Linguistic Inquiry* 19:335–391.
Lee, K. D. 1978. Cotongsa "cita" uy uymi yenkwu. *Hankul* 161:29–61.
Lee, S. O. 1972. Tongsa uy thukseng ey tayhan ihae. *Language Research* 8:44–59.

Lyons, J. 1968. *Introduction to theoretical linguistics.* Cambridge: Cambridge University Press.
———. 1977. *Semantics,* vol. 2. Cambridge: Cambridge University Press.
Masuoka, T. 1982. Nihogo judobun no imi bunseki. *Gengo kenkyuu* 82:48–64.
Matthew, S. D. 1982. In defence of a universal passive. *Linguistic Analysis* 10:53–61.
Mikami, A. 1960. *Zoo wa hana ga nagai.* Tokyo: Kuroshio Shuppan.
Miller, J. 1985. *Semantics and syntax: Parallels and connections.* Cambridge: Cambridge University Press.
Miyagawa, Shigeru. Blocking and Japanese causatives. *Lingua* 64:177–207.
Newmeyer, Frederick J. 1983. *Grammatical theory.* Chicago: University of Chicago Press.
Nishio, H. 1983. Passive and causative in Japanese and elsewhere. *Papers in East Asian Languages* 1:91–99.
Okutsu, Keiichiroo. 1980. Doosi bunkei no hikaku. In *Nichi-ei-go hikaku kooza,* vol. 2, *Bunpoo,* ed. by T. Kunihiro. Tokyo: Taishukan.
———. 1983. Naze ukemi ka? *Kokugogaku* 132:65–80.
Park, Yang-Kyu. 1978. Satong kwa phitong. *Kwukehak* 7:48–70.
Perlmutter, David, and Paul Postal. 1977. Toward a universal characterization of passivization. *Berkeley Linguistic Society* 3:394–417.
Quirk, R., Greenbaum, G. Leech, and J. Svartvik. 1972. *A grammar of contemporary English.* London: Longman.
Ranson, E. N. 1979. Definiteness and animacy constraints on passive and double object constructions in English. *Glossa* 13:215–240.
Sato, C. 1982. Some properties of inanimate subject passives. *Papers in Japanese Linguistics* 8:177–190.
Shibatani, Masayoshi. 1982. Japanese grammar and universal grammar. *Lingua* 57:103–123.
Shibatani, M., T. Kageyama, and I. Tamori. 1982. *Gengo no koozoo-riron to bunseki: Imi toogo hen.* Tokyo: Kuroshio Shuppan.
Shimizu, M. 1975. Relational grammar and promotion rules in Japanese. *Chicago Linguistic Society* 11:529–535.
Shin, G. G. 1981. Exceptions of passivization in Korean. *Ehak* 8:49–68. Cenpuk Tayhakkyo Ehak Yenkwuso.
———. 1982. Passive constructions in Korean. *Ene* 3:199–240.
Suga, Y. 1980. Ukemi no koobun to imi. *Kokugo-kokubun kenkyuu* 63:25–40.
Sung, K. S. 1976. Kwuke uy kancep phitong ey tayhaye. *Munpep yenkwu* 3:159–182.
———. 1981. Thatongseng mokceke wa cwung mokceke. *Emun loncip* 22:115–127.
Teramura, H. 1982. *Nihongo no shintakusu to imi.* Tokyo: Kuroshio Shuppan.
Tokieda, M. 1950. *Nihon bunpoo, koogo hen.* Tokyo: Iwanami.
Wasow, T. 1980. Major and minor rules in lexical grammar. In *Lexical grammar,* ed. by T. Hoekstra, H. van der Hulst, and M. Moortgat. Dordrecht: Foris.

Wierzbicka, A. 1979. Are grammatical categories vague or polysemous? (The Japanese "adversative" passive in a typological context). *Papers in Linguistics* 12:111–164.

Wilkins, Wendy. 1988. *Thematic relations*. New York: Academic Press.

Williams, Edwin. 1980. Predication. *Linguistic Inquiry* 11:203–238.

Yamanaka, N. 1984. Basho shugo bunkei, basho mokutekigo bunkei to imiteki yooin. *Kokugogaku* 139:43–53.

Yom Jong Yul. 1980. *Munhwae hyengthaylon*. Pyongyang: Kim Il Sung University Press.

Yoshida, K. 1971. *Gendaigo jodooshi no shiteki kenkyuu*. Tokyo: Meiji Shoin.